JOHN
LENNON

By the same author

Honky Tonkin' – A Travel Guide To American Music
The Best Of Country Music (with Fred Dellar)
Elvis Presley – The King Of Rock And Roll
The Illustrated Country Almanac
Elvis Presley – The Legend And The Music (with John Tobler)
The Illustrated Book Of Country Music Lists (with Fred Dellar)

JOHN LENNON

RICHARD WOOTTON

HODDER AND STOUGHTON
LONDON SYDNEY AUCKLAND TORONTO

For PAT and MAX
with love and thanks

British Library Cataloguing in Publication Data

Wootton, Richard
  John Lennon. – (Twentieth century people)
  1. Lennon, John   II. Singers – England – Biography –
  Juvenile literature
  I. Title   II. Series
  784.5′0092′4   ML420.L38

   ISBN 0-340-33431-2 (cased)
   ISBN 0-340-358750 (limp)

Text copyright © 1984 Richard Wootton
First published 1984

Published by Hodder and Stoughton Children's Books,
a division of Hodder and Stoughton Ltd,
Mill Road, Dunton Green, Sevenoaks, Kent TN13 2YJ

Printed in Great Britain by
St Edmundsbury Press,
Bury St Edmunds, Suffolk

Photoset by Rowland Phototypesetting Ltd,
Bury St Edmunds, Suffolk.

Contents

Acknowledgements and Thanks

My thanks are due to several authors who have written about the Beatles and John Lennon's life and music. Of particular use have been *Shout! The True Story of the Beatles* by Philip Norman, *John Lennon 1940–1980* by Ray Connolly, *The Beatles, An Illustrated Record* by Roy Carr and Tony Tyler, *The Long and Winding Road – A History of the Beatles on Record* by Neville Stannard and John Tobler, *Lennon Remembers* by Jan Wenner, *John Lennon: One Day at a Time* by Anthony Fawcett, *The Beatles in their Own Words* and *John Lennon in his Own Words* both compiled by Miles, *The Beatles Who's Who* by Bill Harry, *The Beatles Apart* by Bob Woffinden and *The Ballad of John and Yoko* by the editors of *Rolling Stone*.

I've consulted magazine articles and newspaper reports in publications too numerous to mention, but special thanks are due to the *London Standard, Melody Maker, Disc* and *NME* in London and *Rolling Stone* in New York.

Various people helped with the collection of photographs and I'm particularly grateful to Roy Burchall and Dave Howling at *Melody Maker*, Terry Norman at Express Newspapers, Ron Jones and Spencer Leigh in Liverpool, Hunter Davies, Vivien Green, Brian Southall, Kathy Gardner, Jonathan Morrish and Peter O'Brien.

1
The
Early Years

John Lennon was born in the early evening of October 9th 1940 at the Oxford Street Maternity Hospital in Liverpool, England. According to many sources, the birth took place during a particularly violent air raid by bombers of the German Luftwaffe.

Britain was at war with Hitler's Nazi Germany, so John's mother, Julia, decided to give her first-born son the middle name of Winston in honour of the man who was leading the British war effort, Prime Minister Winston Churchill. It was a name which later caused John Lennon considerable embarrassment and in the sixties he changed it by deed poll.

Julia Stanley, one of five sisters, was a dreamy, somewhat scatterbrained and eccentric individual with a quirky sense of humour, traits inherited to an extent by her son. In December 1938 she had married Alfred 'Freddie' Lennon on impulse and much against the wishes of her family.

Freddie came from a family so large and unmanageable that much of his childhood was spent in an orphanage, and he worked, whenever he could get employment, as a ship's waiter. Julia's father, who was an official of a Liverpool salvage company, and sisters didn't like Freddie and considered him irresponsible and unreliable. Their worst fears were confirmed when the marriage failed – Freddie spent much of his time at sea, was absent when John was born and for much of the war, and then completely disappeared for many years, returning only when John was famous.

Despite their opposition to the marriage, Julia's sisters were very kind and helpful when she had the baby, especially Mimi Stanley, who had married a man named George Smith. Mimi had no children of her own and became very fond of John, frequently looking after him when Julia was working or spent an evening out. A new man with children of his own came into Julia Lennon's life and when it became clear that John was not wanted in this new family, the little boy moved in with his Aunt Mimi and Uncle George.

They weren't rich, neither were they poor – upper-working-class is probably an accurate description of their social circumstances. They lived in the Liverpool suburb of Woolton, close to a Salvation Army children's home called Strawberry Field, which provided the inspiration for one of the best-known songs John wrote for the Beatles, 'Strawberry Fields Forever'.

John was brought up by Mimi and George as if he was their own son. He was told little about the troubled background of his parents' marriage, though Julia, whom he called 'Mummy', visited occasionally, travelling the short distance from her home at Spring Wood by bus. Mimi was devoted to John, as she told writer Philip Norman, 'Never a day passed when I wasn't with him – just that one time a year when he went up to Scotland to stay with his cousins. And at night, for ten years, I never crossed the threshold of that house . . . I brought him up strictly.

Above: *John, aged 8, with his mother Julia.*
Right: *John's Aunt Mimi* (both photos from *The Beatles* by Hunter Davies)
Below: *251 Menlove Avenue in Woolton, where John grew up with his Aunt Mimi and Uncle George.* (Richard Wootton)

No sweets – just one barley sugar at night – and no sitting around in picture-dromes.'

At the age of four, John began going to school, Dovedale Primary, which is very near Penny Lane, the Liverpool street later immortalised in the Beatles' song of the same name. One of John's class-mates was Peter Harrison, whose younger brother George began attending the school two years later. John showed early promise; he learnt to read quickly and was good at creative writing and art work. Some of the crayon drawings from his time at Dovedale Primary were featured on the cover of his 1974 solo LP, 'Walls And Bridges'.

John liked sport, especially swimming and athle-tics, but he performed poorly in games like football, due to poor eyesight. At home he enjoyed writing stories and magazines for his own amusement, fre-quently changing words for comic effect. He was an avid reader and among his favourite fictional charac-ters was the mischievous but lovable hero of Richmal Crompton's *Just William* books. John was like Wil-liam in many ways, often in trouble with his gang of friends, Pete Shotton, Ivan Vaughan and Nigel Whalley. He took sweets from shops, played frighten-ing 'dare' games and generally annoyed people, though at home with his aunt and uncle he was invariably well-behaved, polite and quiet.

Pete Shotton and John Lennon became virtually inseparable and both attended the same secondary school, Quarry Bank Grammar, from 1952. They showed considerable academic potential but, after beginning well, slipped to the 'C' stream, which was below their level. John became the clown of his class; loved by his fellow schoolboys but loathed by the

Quarry Bank Grammar School (now a Comprehensive) where John was a pupil between 1952 and 1957. (Richard Wootton)

teachers for disrupting the lessons. The school punishment book reveals a long and varied list of misdemeanours, including 'throwing a blackboard duster out of window' and 'gambling on school field'. Aunt Mimi, on her own now since the death of George Smith when John was twelve, received regular complaints from the school about her nephew's truanting and bad behaviour.

While the ever-caring and patient Mimi did her best to keep John under control, Julia Lennon behaved very differently towards the boy. Pete Shotton has recalled how he accompanied John on visits to his mother and that they'd frequently find Julia doing unusual things. 'She'd do tricks to make us laugh, like wearing glasses with no glass in the frames, then putting her finger through the frames to wipe her eyes.' Julia's attitude to life was to 'live for the day' and not to worry about the future, so she didn't get cross with John when she heard that he'd skipped lessons. Where Mimi would have been angry, Julia just laughed.

Significantly, perhaps, it was Julia who first got John playing a musical instrument, as he recalled years later; 'I started with a banjo when I was fifteen, when my mother taught me some banjo chords.' But music didn't become particularly important until a year later, in 1956, when John Lennon heard Elvis Presley's first hit record. 'We never listened to pop music in our house, but when I heard "Heartbreak Hotel" I thought, "This is it." Nothing really affected me until Elvis.'

It is difficult today to imagine just how dramatic an effect Elvis and rock 'n' roll had on young people in the mid-fifties. Until then popular music had been aimed at an older audience, with singers who dressed smartly, stood still by the microphone as they sang and smiled at the fans. But almost everything about Elvis was different – he wore garish clothes, moved frantically and snarled at his audiences. Though Presley shocked most adults, for teenagers like John Lennon he was an exciting new hero. Elvis inspired John to form his first musical group and provided him with a means to channel his rebellion into something constructive.

Though Elvis Presley was the biggest rock 'n' roll star, a British performer, named Lonnie Donegan, was much easier to imitate. Lonnie's rock-'n'-roll-influenced music was called 'skiffle' and could be performed with cheap guitars and home-made in-struments, like a washboard strummed with thimbles for percussive effect.

Elvis Presley.
(RCA Records)

John formed a skiffle group, the Quarrymen (named after his school), with his great friend, Peter Shotton. John played guitar, Peter the washboard, and a variety of people played other instruments, including Ivan Vaughan and Nigel Whalley (still friends with John though neither attended Quarry Bank school) who alternated on the one-string tea-chest bass. The group performed several American folk songs which had been popularised by Lonnie Donegan, including 'Cumberland Gap' and 'Railroad Bill', and American rock 'n' roll songs, like Wanda Jackson's 'Let's Have A Party'. The Quarrymen would dearly have loved to sing Elvis' material, but the singer's early hits were so echoey that they were difficult to imitate successfully, though the breathless, energetic way in which Presley sang did influence John's own vocal performance.

'I used to borrow a guitar at first,' John recalled, years later, 'I couldn't play but a pal of mine had one and it fascinated me. Eventually my mother bought me one from one of those mail-order firms. I suppose it was a bit crummy, when you think about it. But I played it all the time and I got a lot of practice.'

The beginnings of the Beatles can be traced from the very amateurish first line-ups of the Quarrymen. The musicians in the group changed around a lot and one of the newcomers was a young lad called Paul McCartney, who went to school with Ivan Vaughan.

Paul came along to what is generally regarded as the group's first important public performance, at the St Peter's Church fete in Woolton on June 15th 1956. The Quarrymen played on a raised platform and had a large crowd, it being a sunny day. Paul was impressed by the group, but particularly by John. After the performance Paul demonstrated his skills by singing and playing Eddie Cochran's rock 'n' roll hit, 'Twenty Flight Rock'.

John Lennon was instantly attracted to Paul because he was a much better musician than any of his schoolmates, could sing, and 'looked like Elvis'. Having weighed up the various pros and cons of Paul (including the obvious danger that he might challenge John as leader of the group) Lennon invited McCartney to join the Quarrymen.

Paul McCartney was two years younger than John, born in Liverpool on June 18th 1942, but was already well ahead of his new friend musically, being able to play the guitar and already writing songs. He inspired John to begin writing and the world-famous songwriting partnership of Lennon and McCartney started from these early meetings in the second half of 1956. They began composing separately, but then helped each other to polish and shape a song to completion. One of John's earliest compositions was entitled 'One After 909', though it wasn't recorded for over ten years and eventually appeared on the Beatles' 1970 LP, 'Let It Be'.

Paul came from a working-class background; his father Jim McCartney was a poorly paid cotton salesman who scrimped and saved to provide Paul, and his younger son Michael, with the education and opportunities that he'd been denied. When John and Paul first met, Jim McCartney was bringing up his sons alone, his wife Mary having died of cancer in early 1956. He'd been in a jazz band in the twenties and encouraged Paul's interest in music, though he had ambitions for his son to become a teacher. Paul and John met regularly in the front room of the McCartney house, when Jim was at work, to practise and to play records.

The two teenagers got on well together, though they had very different personalities. Paul was generally hard-working, calm and even-tempered, but John was frequently lazy, reckless and quick to anger. Paul had a charm and politeness which endeared him to adults, where John had a rebellious nature which often antagonised people; but these outward appearances were deceptive, because though John seemed tough, he was soft and sensitive at heart, while Paul, though seemingly very easy-

15

going, could be very hard and stubborn and was businesslike in his approach to music making. Nigel Whalley, who'd changed from being a member of the Quarrymen to acting as a kind of manager, recalls that Paul gave him a hard time about the amount of money he was getting for the band's occasional performances at church hall social functions.

By the second half of 1957, John Lennon and Paul McCartney were seeing each other on a daily basis. John was attending the Liverpool Art College and Paul was at the nearby Liverpool Institute school. John had left Quarry Bank Grammar in the summer of 1957, having failed all eight of his O-level examinations. The school recommended a career as an artist because art seemed to be the only subject he was interested in. Mimi agreed to support John financially while he attended art school, and hoped he'd do better than at Quarry Bank.

The Liverpool Art College (now part of the Liverpool Polytechnic) which John attended from 1957. The building in the background (with pillars) is the Liverpool Institute, where George Harrison and Paul McCartney were both students. (Richard Wootton)

Two early influences on John and Paul were American rock 'n' roll musicians like Jerry Lee Lewis – above left, and Carl Perkins – above right. (Elektra and Sun Records)

John did not work hard at his art studies, but concentrated instead on making music. The Quarrymen were improving musically and were now playing rock 'n' roll material exclusively, because the skiffle phase was over. Liverpool was probably the best place in England for rock 'n' roll enthusiasts because the city was Europe's busiest transatlantic passenger port and the seamen who regularly made the trip to New York returned with the latest American records (including many that weren't otherwise available in the UK). Discs by the likes of Little Richard, Jerry Lee Lewis and Carl Perkins, which John and Paul heard at Liverpool parties and social functions, were an important influence on the growing repertoire of the Quarrymen and the songwriting of Lennon and McCartney.

In 1958 Paul introduced John to George Harrison, a fourteen-year-old student at the Liverpool Institute. George, the son of a bus driver, was another rock 'n' roll fan and had taught himself to play the guitar by listening to Buddy Holly records over and over again. John became a hero for George, but Lennon was not immediately impressed by the scruffy teenager, who was three years his junior. 'I couldn't be bothered with him when he first came around,' John recalled in an interview, years later. 'He used to follow me round like a kid, hanging around all the time.'

George accompanied John and Paul wherever they went and was eventually allowed to make occasional guest appearances with the Quarrymen. He had a £30 guitar, which was a much better instrument than the one Paul played, and it soon became obvious that he was a good musician and should be playing lead guitar with the group. He became a regular member of the Quarrymen, edging out Eric Griffiths, who'd been one of the founders. Pete Shotton had also left by this time, but remained a very close friend of John's.

Paul, George and John were now the nucleus of the band, even wearing a stage 'uniform' of fashionable drain-pipe trousers, white cowboy shirts and black bootlace ties. They didn't have a regular drummer, as John later explained to American writer Jan Wenner, 'We had different drummers all the time, because people who owned drum kits were few and far between; it was an expensive item. They were usually idiots!'

In the summer of 1958, tragedy came suddenly into the life of 17-year-old John Lennon. On July 15th 1958 his mother was run over and killed by a car, while she was on her way home from visiting Mimi. John did not show undue grief at the time, but in retrospect we know that he was terribly hurt and upset, and in some ways never properly recovered from the loss.

As a baby John had been rejected, first by his father, then by his mother, though in his teens he had formed a relationship of sorts with Julia – more like a big-sister friendship than anything else; but now she had left him again, and this time for good.

Julia Lennon's sudden death marked a turning point in John's life. It made him very angry and hardened him; making him frequently bitter and aggressive towards other people. He was popular at art school because of his unusual sense of humour, but he was the kind of person it is better to know casually than to be close friends with. John was often very unkind and cruel to those around him, particularly girl friends.

The memory of his mother remained strongly with John throughout his life and it's significant that he named his first son Julian, that he wrote a beautiful song about her, 'Julia' (which appeared on 'The Beatles', the white double LP of 1968), and often called Yoko, the older woman who became his second wife, 'mother'.

2
The
Silver Beatles

John made two special and important friends at art college – Cynthia Powell and Stuart Sutcliffe. Cynthia was in the same lettering class and was a very conventional, quiet and mild-mannered person – almost the complete opposite of the rowdy and unorthodox John Lennon; yet the pair were soon 'going steady'. John had several girl friends before Cynthia, but all the relationships had been short-lived because the girls were put off by his selfish behaviour and rudeness. Cynthia was more resilient and, despite what her better instincts may have told her, was completely enamoured of John, though she frequently found him very difficult and even frightening.

He was extremely protective and became very jealous when other boys paid attention to her. Years later Cynthia recalled, in her autobiography *A Twist Of Lennon*, that, 'John's jealousy and possessiveness were at times unbearable, and I found myself a quaking, nervous wreck on many occasions. His moods were totally unpredictable; his temper and language were savage.'

John met Stuart Sutcliffe, the other friend, at Ye Cracke, a pub in Rice Street which was popular with students and just around the corner from the Liverpool Art Institute. A pale and rather unhealthy-

Stuart Sutcliffe – John Lennon's closest male friend. He was bass guitarist for the Beatles between 1959 and 1961. (Popperfoto)

looking young man, Stu was probably the most gifted and promising artist at the college while John was the laziest and the least enthusiastic. They both stood out from the crowd because their clothes were very different from the other students'. Stu had his own unique style; he favoured very tight trousers, high-sided boots and brightly coloured shirts. John was the college's only 'teddy boy'; sporting narrow 'drain-pipe' trousers and pointed 'winkle-picker' shoes. Stu was amused by Lennon's eccentric behaviour and comic writings – he carried scraps of paper with him containing strange drawings and funny poems; and John became fascinated by Sutcliffe's talk of paint-ings and art. For the first time he was encouraged to

21

take a serious interest in art, though this did not have a significant effect on his studies.

Stu was not a musician but was soon very interested in the activities of the Quarrymen. When he won an art competition he invested the £65 prize money on a Hoffner President bass guitar, and then joined John's group. Lennon did his best to teach Sutcliffe how to play the instrument, and in return Stu introduced John to his favourite artists. Stu never became very adept at playing the bass guitar and at concerts stood with his back to the audience so that people couldn't see what he was doing.

It was 1959 and the Quarrymen continued to perform whenever they got the chance, though that wasn't too often as they weren't particularly impressive – they frequently lacked a drummer and didn't have very good equipment (apart from Stu's classy bass which was of little value as he played it so badly).

The group rarely earned more than a couple of pounds for a night's work, sometimes performing at church hall dances, once at the bus depot where George's dad worked, and at the Casbah Coffee Club in West Derby. This club was in the basement of a large Victorian guest house owned by Mona Best. She'd cleared out the dark cellar to make a social centre for her sons, Rory and Pete.

The Quarrymen played at the opening night of the Casbah, which soon became very popular and successful. Pete Best, a shy boy who was reluctant to push himself forward, was inspired by the musicians who played at the club to buy a drum kit and when the Quarrymen moved on to bigger and better things, he started his own band there, called the Blackjacks.

Paul and John were becoming increasingly ambitious for their band and they even wrote a press handout which claimed Paul was 'reading English at Liverpool University', that they'd written more than fifty songs, played with a 'jazz feel' and performed standards like 'Ain't She Sweet' and 'You Are My Sunshine'.

In June they were given an audition for the 'Carroll Levis TV Discoveries' talent show. They travelled to Manchester for a regional heat and introduced themselves as Johnny and the Moondogs, a name that Lennon now considered more suitable for a rock 'n' roll band.

The name change didn't help and they failed the audition, but returned to Liverpool undeterred and changed their name again, at Stu Sutcliffe's suggestion, to the Beetles, a title apparently inspired by the insect name adopted by Buddy Holly's group, the Crickets. John, who could never resist playing with words, changed it to the Beatles. Shortly afterwards they decided to make themselves sound grander, and became the Silver Beatles.

It was with this name that they met their first professional manager, Allan Williams, who was the owner of the Jacaranda coffee bar, which was a popular meeting place for Liverpool students. Williams booked bands into the cellar below the bar and initially hired the Silver Beatles to paint murals on the walls, then began booking them to play at lunchtime sessions.

Early in 1960, Larry Parnes, a concert promoter and manager from London, came to Liverpool and asked Allan Williams to arrange an audition of the best local groups so that he could find a suitable band to back the popular singer, Billy Fury. The Silver Beatles were among the acts on display, with a friend, Johnny Hutchinson, sitting in on drums. Parnes liked what he heard but asked them to perform again without Stu Sutcliffe, who he'd noticed didn't seem able to play the bass. John refused to leave his friend out of the group so they lost the chance of a tour with Fury, but in the spring they were offered a job supporting another of Larry Parnes' acts, singer Johnny Gentle.

The tour of the north of England was, by all accounts, harrowing and depressing. There were long and tedious journeys between concert halls, and they travelled together in the back of a cramped van with all the equipment. Their temporary drummer, Tommy Moore, who was several years older than the others, was particularly horrified by the experience and quit soon afterwards, but John, Paul, George and Stu retained their strong ambitions to be pop musicians and continued to look for bookings. Allan Williams became their manager and arranged for them to play at dances in the Liverpool area, alongside other up-and-coming young groups like Gerry and the Pacemakers.

Fights were frequent occurrences at these dances and one night, at the Litherland Town Hall, the Silver Beatles were ambushed as they left the building. Stu Sutcliffe was knocked to the ground and, before the others could rescue him, was kicked savagely in the head. He did not see a doctor and the incident is now thought to have contributed to his tragic death two years later.

Paul and George left school in the summer of 1960, McCartney having passed one A-level exam, in art.

George began working as an electrician, but Paul couldn't find suitable work. At the same time John was asked to leave the art college because he had done so little work. He didn't immediately tell his long-suffering Aunt Mimi, with whom he still lived in Woolton.

The future didn't look very bright for the band: they were drummerless again and getting fewer bookings. Then, in August, Allan Williams managed to get them a job playing in a club in the West German city of Hamburg. Aunt Mimi was shocked to hear this news, also to discover that John had been thrown out of art college, and was only partially pacified when her nephew said he'd be earning '£100 a week'. Paul and George both got permission from their parents, though Stu nearly didn't go because he was due to begin a teacher-training course. The group still needed a drummer, so Paul McCartney approached Pete Best at the Casbah Club and offered him the job, which he readily accepted.

Allan Williams gave them money to buy a band 'uniform' (these were days when professional pop groups invariably dressed alike), including tennis shoes, roll-neck sweaters and high buttoned jackets. They were very excited when they set off from Liverpool in Allan's Austin minibus, but the journey was long and hard and their welcome in Germany wasn't particularly warm. The Indra Club, which was owned by Williams' Hamburg associate, Bruno Koschmeider, was small and dingy and the group discovered they were expected to play for up to six hours a night. Their sleeping quarters were behind the screen of a cinema owned by Bruno, and they didn't have proper beds. After a late night the young musicians had the chance of only a few hours' sleep before being awakened by the deafening noise of the first film.

The group hated everything about Germany to start with, but things improved when they met some of the other Liverpool groups who were playing in Hamburg clubs in the Reeperbahn district and after a few weeks they became popular with the local music fans and Bruno moved them to a bigger club, the Kaiserkeller, where they alternated with another Merseyside group, Rory Storm and the Hurricanes, whose drummer was a young man named Richard Starkey, though he preferred to be known as Ringo Starr.

Among the new fans in Hamburg were a couple from the local art school; Klaus Voorman, an illustrator, and Astrid Kirchnerr, a designer. Astrid and Stu Sutcliffe fell in love. She had a lot of money and bought him high fashion clothes, which the others mocked, but then she gave him a new hair style – the hair combed forward without a parting – which they liked, and Astrid did the same for all of them, except Pete Best. Thus was born the Beatles haircut, which later became world-famous. Two months after they had first met, Astrid and Stu became engaged.

The Beatles, as they now called themselves, were working long hours for pitiful wages. Then a new club opened in Hamburg called the Top Ten, and the owner Peter Eckhorn offered them better money and proper sleeping accommodation, so they quit the Kaiserkeller. Bruno was furious and reported them to the police, who discovered that George Harrison was seventeen and too young to be working in the clubs. He was deported, and then Pete Best and Paul McCartney were arrested on a bizarre charge of setting light to some curtains at their old lodging place. A few days later they returned to England, followed by John, who made the journey by train with as much of their equipment as he could carry, and Stu, who was bought a plane ticket by Astrid's family. The Beatles had been in Germany for five months and returned to a cold Liverpool in December 1960, penniless.

John went back to his Aunt Mimi's house and was so exhausted that he spent a whole week in bed. His aunt told him off for wasting time and suggested that he get a proper job. Paul McCartney received a similar lecture and began a short-lived job as a delivery boy. The Beatles didn't play for a couple of weeks, but were then booked for a dance at the Litherland Town Hall, two days after Christmas. Their old friends

OPERATION BIG BEAT

TOWER BALLROOM, NEW BRIGHTON

FRIDAY, 10th NOVEMBER, 1961   7-30 A.M.—1-0 A.M.
JIVING TO MERSEYSIDE'S TOP 5 GROUPS
THE BEATLES————————GERRY AND THE PACEMAKERS
RORY STORM AND THE HURRICANES————————THE REMO FOUR
KINGSIZE TAYLOR AND THE DOMINOES

LATE TRANSPORT   L. CHESHIRE) TWO LICENSED BARS (until 11-30 pm.)   BUFFET
TICKETS 5/- from   s and Tower Ballroom.   Transport details from Agencies and Crown Coachways and
Mersey Tunnel, Manchester Street from 7-0 p.m onwards

LITHERLAND TOWN HALL

EVERY THURSDAY

THE MAGNIFICENT

BEATLES !!

JOHN, PAUL, GEORGE AND PETE

ALWAYS A

Lively Time Here
Litherland Town Hall

YOUR THURSDAY DANCE DATE

Two newspaper advertisements for concerts featuring 'The Beatles' in 1961. Note the line-up then included Pete Best.

were astonished by the group's performance, because they had improved almost out of recognition. Their gruelling six-hour sets in Hamburg had moulded them into a professional and entertaining group.

In the audience was a man named Bob Wooler, a local disc jockey, who was so impressed that he began helping them to get other bookings. Also present was Neil Aspinall, who disliked rock 'n' roll and had only come along because he was a friend of Pete Best's brother, but he liked the Beatles so much that soon afterwards he was helping them at all their shows, loading and setting up equipment.

In 1961 Bob Wooler began hosting lunchtime rock 'n' roll sessions at the Cavern Club, a cramped, almost airless basement at 10 Matthew Street in the centre of Liverpool, which featured jazz groups each evening. He persuaded the club's owner, Ray McFall, to book the Beatles. They were successful and drew a large crowd of local office workers. All the musicians were officially unemployed and drawing dole money, but they earned 25 shillings (£1-25) a day, four lunchtimes a week.

Their repertoire, remembered fondly by Cavern Club regulars including Bob, and the cloakroom girl Priscilla White (later a successful singer, Cilla Black), was a glorious mixture of rock 'n' roll songs, like Little Richard's 'Good Golly Miss Molly', show tunes, like 'Till There Was You', and their own originals, including 'Hello Little Girl', one of the first songs written by John Lennon.

Paul and John would stand together at the front, playing their guitars and singing, frequently sharing the same microphone; George stood solemnly at the side, concentrating on his playing; Stu Sutcliffe continued to perform with his back to the audience; and the reticent Pete Best sat astride his drum stool, the focal point of most female eyes in the club, because, at this stage, the attractive young man was the most popular member of the Beatles.

Stu Sutcliffe realised that he would never make a proper musician and was on the verge of leaving the group. He was still close friends with John but was aware that Paul McCartney actively disliked his presence and wanted to take over on the bass guitar.

In April 1961, the Beatles accepted the offer of another trip to Hamburg, to play at the Top Ten club. They were keen to return because some of their equipment, including Pete Best's favourite drum kit, was still in the city, and they'd been promised better money than they'd received before. They were still expected to play long hours, but they had real work permits (George was now eighteen and therefore 'legal') and better living conditions.

Stu decided to make the trip with them because he wanted to be reunited with his beloved Astrid. She persuaded him to enrol at Hamburg's art school, where the authorities welcomed him with open arms because he was such a gifted artist. After a month of combining art in the daytime with music at night, Stu left the band, lending his bass guitar to Paul, who eagerly took over the role of bassist, while George concentrated on lead guitar and John played rhythm.

In June 1961, Stu married Astrid and lived with her in Hamburg, all the while keeping in contact with John by exchanging long and personal letters, until he died, tragically, of a brain haemorrhage on April 10th 1962. He was just twenty-one. John was very sad and upset by the death of Stuart Sutcliffe, the closest and most important male friend in his life.

The second trip to Hamburg, which lasted three months, was significant as the first time the Beatles made a commercial recording. Bert Kaempfert, the German orchestra leader and record producer, came to the Top Ten club and saw the Beatles playing with another British artist, singer Tony Sheridan. Bert assumed that they were all in the same band and signed them up to make a record. The Beatles cut eight tracks, six involving them playing behind Tony Sheridan's vocals, but two were on their own: 'Ain't She Sweet', which marked John's recording debut as a lead singer, and the instrumental 'Cry For A Shadow'. Bert Kaempfert's productions with his own orchestra have brought huge sales and deserved success, but his work with the Beatles was poor and gives no clue to the group's special talent or later success.

A single from the session, 'My Bonnie', was released and became successful in Germany. The song featured Tony Sheridan with the Beatles providing musical and vocal support, plus hand-clapping, a sound they utilised very successfully on their own records.

The Beatles returned to Liverpool with a few copies of 'My Bonnie' on the German Polydor label and they gave one to Bob Wooler, who began playing it regularly at the Cavern Club. The closest record shop to the club was the North East Music Store (NEMS), which was managed by a man named Brian Epstein. He became puzzled by requests for 'My Bonnie', the first, according to his autobiography *A Cellarful of Noise*, coming on Saturday October 21st 1961 from a regular customer named Raymond Jones. When Brian discovered that the Beatles played regularly at lunchtimes in the Cavern Club, he decided to investigate.

Epstein found the club 'dark, damp and smelly', and immediately regretted coming, but then saw the featured group: 'I had never seen anything like the Beatles on any stage,' he wrote later. 'They smoked as they played and they ate and talked and pretended to hit each other ... But they gave a captivating and honest show and they had very considerable magnetism.'

Brian was also impressed by their music and went backstage after their show to talk to them. Without really knowing why, he invited them to come to his store one afternoon, 'just for a chat'. Back at the shop he ordered 100 copies of 'My Bonnie' from Germany, and by the scheduled time of their meeting, had sold them all.

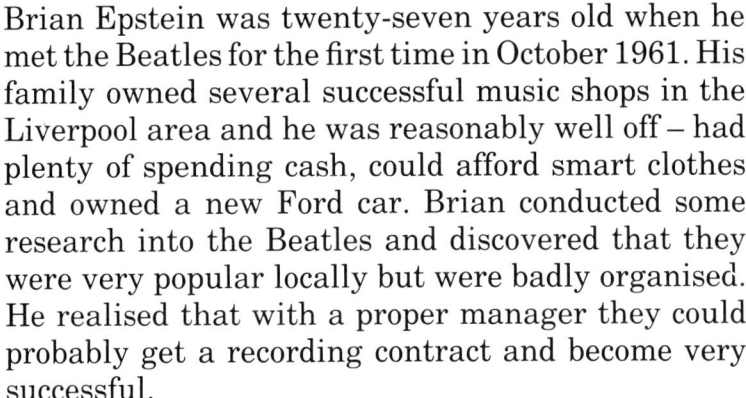

3
From Liverpool to London

Brian Epstein was twenty-seven years old when he met the Beatles for the first time in October 1961. His family owned several successful music shops in the Liverpool area and he was reasonably well off – had plenty of spending cash, could afford smart clothes and owned a new Ford car. Brian conducted some research into the Beatles and discovered that they were very popular locally but were badly organised. He realised that with a proper manager they could probably get a recording contract and become very successful.

His prearranged chat with the Beatles established that they were serious about a career in music and, although they initially annoyed him by turning up late, he offered to become their manager. They asked only that he didn't try and change their musical style, a condition that he readily agreed to, then said 'yes' to his terms. Brian actually knew very little about being the manager of a pop group, but he took advice from a family solicitor. The Beatles trusted him because of his professional manner and the fact that he had money. 'He looked efficient and rich,' John said later.

It was harder to convince the parents and guardians, John's Aunt Mimi proving, typically, to be the most obstinate. She didn't believe that John could make a living as a musician, but Brian promised to pay special attention to her nephew and to ensure that he wouldn't suffer in any way. 'He's the only important one,' Mimi recalled Brian telling her, 'I'll always take care of John.'

Others, who knew Epstein well, agree that John Lennon was by far the most important Beatle in his eyes and the main reason that he'd taken the group on. After the numerous teachers and art school lecturers that had dismissed Lennon as lazy and worthless, Brian was the first person with power and influence to recognise his true potential.

The NEMS shops which were owned by Brian's family were important customers with the big, London-based record companies and Epstein used the name to get an audition for his band, forming a company called NEMS Enterprises.

Decca Records, which released hits by popular singers Tommy Steele and Billy Fury, were the first to show a serious interest in the four musicians, sending a man to Liverpool to watch the Beatles perform at the Cavern Club. He was sufficiently impressed to ask Brian to bring the group to London to make some demonstration recordings.

The Beatles came to the Decca Studios on January 1st 1962 and went through their stage act, performing a wide-ranging selection of songs which included rock 'n' roll songs made famous by other people, pop standards and some of their own compositions.

Decca was not very impressed by the tape, and copies which have subsequently appeared on illegal 'bootleg' records make the lack of enthusiasm understandable – the performance gave little indication of the Beatles' talent. A Decca representative told

John Lennon

Helen Shapiro, the popular British singer with whom the Beatles toured in 1963. (EMI Records)

Brian Epstein that the company wouldn't be signing his group, adding, rather unkindly that 'groups with guitars are on the way out', an opinion presumably based on the chart domination of the time by solo singers like Cliff Richard and Helen Shapiro. Brian was astonished, 'You must be out of your mind,' he said. 'These boys are going to explode. I am completely convinced that one day they will be bigger than Elvis Presley.'

Brian subsequently took copies of the demo tape to other record companies in London. Meanwhile, the Beatles were back in Liverpool where their popularity was growing in leaps and bounds. When the local music paper, *Mersey Beat*, conducted a poll to find the most popular band, the Beatles were easy winners.

The group was now better than ever musically and, thanks to Brian's management, had adopted a more professional attitude to their work – they had become much more punctual, wore smarter clothes and had stopped smoking and swearing while on stage.

By May 1962, Epstein had been turned down by almost every big record company and was on the point of giving up when someone suggested that he approach producer George Martin, who ran the EMI-owned Parlophone label, which was best known for its comedy records by Peter Sellers. Martin was not over-impressed by the tape but he agreed to give the Beatles an audition.

They were in Germany again, on a Hamburg club engagement which Brian had arranged for much better pay than before, when they received a telegram from Epstein which read CONGRATULATIONS BOYS. EMI REQUEST RECORDING SESSIONS. PLEASE REHEARSE NEW MATERIAL.

The Beatles' second London studio session took place in June, and George Martin used the occasion to test each member of the band individually, mainly because he was looking for the Beatle who could be the frontman (as all groups at the time had one obvious leader), but soon realised that John and Paul were equally strong and it was best to leave them as they were. The one change that he decided to make was with the drummer – Pete Best wasn't good enough to record. Martin planned to use a studio drummer if he signed the Beatles, but the other three had already decided to drop Pete from the group.

According to Brian Epstein, 'The Beatles, both in Hamburg and at home, had decided his beat was wrong for the music. Though he was friendly with John, he was not liked by George and Paul.' They couldn't bring themselves to tell Best, so Brian was given the unpleasant task of sacking him. They chose

Ringo Starr, their friend from Rory Storm's group in the Hamburg days, to be the new drummer.

The sacking of Pete Best caused a controversy among the fans in Liverpool and there were some ugly scenes. George Harrison received a black eye in a fight defending Ringo. Brian told them that they shouldn't worry, their futures lay beyond the horizons of Liverpool and their recording contract was almost assured. In July he signed a contract with EMI and the first proper recording session was planned for September.

August 1962 was a busy month; Ringo made his debut and was introduced to the band's large repertoire of songs, and the Beatles were filmed for the first time, on-stage at the Cavern singing 'Some Other Guy', by a crew from the Manchester-based Granada TV.

Later that month John Lennon was married, after the discovery that his long-time girl friend, Cynthia Powell, had become pregnant. 'I was a bit shocked when she told me,' John recalled later, 'but I said "Yes, we'll have to get married." When I told my Aunt Mimi she just let out a groan.'

John was very fond of Cynthia but had not planned to marry her because he feared it would end his career, 'I thought it would be goodbye to the group, getting married, because everybody said it would be. We went mad keeping it a secret. None of us ever took any girls to the Cavern because we thought we would lose fans, which turned out to be a farce in the end.'

The wedding, at Mount Pleasant Registry Office on August 23rd, was a very quiet affair and was kept a secret from the fans and press. Brian Epstein was the best man and the reception was held at the Reeces

George, Paul, John and Ringo rehearsing at the Cavern in 1962 after Ringo Starr's first appearance. (Peter Kaye Photography)

Cafe, where the couple were toasted in water because the premises didn't have a licence to serve alcohol.

John's Aunt Mimi didn't attend the wedding and didn't talk to her nephew for several weeks, but eventually Cynthia brought about a reconciliation between them, and later they moved into the bottom floor of Mimi's house. The two women came to spend a lot of time together because John was so often away working, even after his son Julian was born, on April 8th 1963.

The Beatles went to the EMI studios in Abbey Road, North London, to record their first Parlophone single on September 11th 1962. The chosen A-side was a Lennon and McCartney song entitled 'Love Me Do', which featured John on lead vocals and a distinctive harmonica solo. The group made seventeen separate recordings of the song before George Martin was satisfied with a version good enough to release. The single appeared, with 'P.S. I Love You' on the B-side, on October 5th.

There were substantial sales in the Merseyside area and it then began picking up national radio plays. By the beginning of November it was in the British charts, reaching a high spot of number 17. It was a modest but very encouraging start for a new group and George Martin called them back to the studio to record the follow-up, 'Please Please Me', which featured John again on lead vocal. They were on top form and this time needed only one take to get it right. 'Gentlemen,' George Martin told them, 'you have just made your first number 1.'

After this November recording session, the Beatles played some more dates in Liverpool, then departed

The Beatles at EMI studios with producer George Martin. (EMI Records)

to Germany for their last appearance at the Star Club in Hamburg. They were very annoyed at having to go, but a contract had been signed in the summer when no-one realised that success would come to them so quickly.

They had a miserable Christmas and New Year in Germany, then returned to England for the release of their second single, which entered the pop charts at the end of January and quickly climbed to number 2.

There was now a demand for a Beatles LP and George Martin had to work fast. His original idea was to record a live album at the Cavern Club, but this proved difficult to organise, so he brought the Beatles to London and asked them to perform a cross-section of material from their live show.

On February 11th they took part in an exhausting sixteen-hour session in which they managed to cut more than enough songs for an LP. It was a remarkable achievement, even in those simplistic early days of LP recording, to cut such a good record so quickly, and so cheaply – the cost to EMI was just £400.

The importance of the Beatles' musical apprenticeship in Germany could now be seen. They had tremendous reserves of energy and could keep playing well for hours on end, and they had a wealth of material – over 100 Lennon and McCartney compositions plus many songs by other people. If they had been 'discovered' earlier, it is unlikely that they would have developed the resources that were to make them so good.

The Beatles' first LP was a very successful and pioneering record. It reached the top spot of the LP charts on May 8th and stayed there for over six months, eventually giving way to their second album, 'With The Beatles'. The album charts had previously been dominated by American releases: Elvis Presley records, plus film soundtracks and comedy albums. Henceforth it would be mainly rock bands and singers.

'Please Please Me', which featured an arresting colour photograph of the Beatles looking down from the central staircase at EMI House in London, contained fourteen songs; excellent value for money at a time when most albums contained ten or twelve. Eight of the songs were written by John and Paul, the remainder being cover versions of American recordings that they particularly liked, including 'Twist And Shout', one of the highlights and closing numbers of their stage show.

The success of the Beatles inspired considerable interest in the other musicians working in Liverpool and there were several stories in the music papers about the supposed 'Liverpool Scene'. Brian Epstein's rapidly expanding NEMS Enterprises looked after several of the most successful acts, including Gerry and the Pacemakers, who'd worked with the Beatles on several occasions; Cilla Black, the former Cavern Club cloakroom girl; and Billy J. Kramer, who worked with a Manchester band called the Dakotas.

Meanwhile the number of people working with the Beatles began to grow, including Dick James, a music publisher who set up the company Northern Songs to administer the songwriting royalties due to John and Paul; Tony Barrow, a journalist who handled their publicity; and Mal Evans who became roadie, taking over from Neil Aspinall who was now their personal assistant.

The Beatles were kept very busy during 1963.

Gerry and the Pacemakers. (EMI Records)

There were numerous concerts and several radio and TV appearances. In February they were on tour with the British girl singer Helen Shapiro. The Beatles were the support act but it soon became clear that most of the audience had come to see them, because they were still screaming their names during Helen's performance. Similar things happened when they were booked to support the popular American star Chris Montez. Halfway through they changed places and the Beatles were top of the bill.

No-one would ever be able to follow them on stage again. They were on an unstoppable course for the top. In early March they cut their third single, 'From Me To You', a song John and Paul had written together on the coach taking them between dates on the Helen Shapiro tour. The single entered the charts at number 6 and the following week was number 1. Their next ten singles would all go straight to the top. It was the beginning of a golden period that was quite unprecedented in the history of popular music.

4
Beatlemania

Within the space of twelve months the Beatles went from being the best loved group in Liverpool to the most popular band in the UK. In May and June 1963 they were top of the singles chart with 'From Me To You' and continued to have the number 1 album.

The other best-selling singles of the period were 'How Do You Do It' by Gerry and the Pacemakers, and the Lennon and McCartney song 'Do You Want To Know A Secret' performed by Billy J. Kramer. Both records had been produced by George Martin at EMI and both acts were managed by Brian Epstein.

The Beatles and their Liverpool musician friends had captured the imagination of the teenage record-buying public and were beginning to attract a far wider audience, encompassing all ages.

The popular newspapers were fascinated by John, Paul, George and Ringo, who always seemed cheerful and ready with an amusing remark or comment, which included their use of Liverpool slang words like 'gear' (great) and 'fab' (fabulous), the latter earning them the nickname of 'The Fab Four'. They had a down-to-earth honesty and a naive charm which appealed to the normally hard-to-please London journalists.

Maureen Cleave of the *Evening Standard*, who wrote the first article on the group for a London

The Beatles, in matching suits, pose for a record company promotional photograph. (EMI Records)

newspaper, said later, 'The Beatles made me laugh immoderately . . . They all had this wonderful quality – it wasn't innocence, but everything was new to them.'

The early sixties was a time of great social change in Britain; an era when it ceased to be necessary for people in important 'top' jobs to come from wealthy backgrounds – the BBC stopped requiring announcers to speak with pronounced middle-class accents; fashion magazines used girls from ordinary backgrounds as models; novels with working-class heroes were in vogue and actors with broad regional accents became major film stars. The Beatles, with their distinctive Liverpool accents and obvious working-class background, were closely identified with these changes.

A new satirical magazine called *Private Eye* and a BBC TV show 'That Was The Week That Was' made it fashionable to be anti-authority and to mock the establishment, so the Beatles' carefree, irreverent attitude to life was also in keeping with the times.

Ray Connolly, a writer who followed the career of the Beatles from the earliest days, has correctly pointed out that the group, especially John Lennon, arrived at just the right moment in time: 'All his life Lennon had been bucking authority, lampooning the establishment, out of step with authority and been chastised for it. Now suddenly his attitude was not only respectable but the very height of fashion.'

By the summer the Beatles were frequently pictured in the popular press and were widely imitated. They changed the look of young Englishmen, who began growing their hair longer and combing it forward into the Beatle-style which had been invented by Astrid Kirchnerr in Hamburg, and copies of their distinctive clothes, including collarless jackets, tab-collared shirts and Cuban boots with thick, high heels, were on sale in high street shops up and down Britain.

The Beatles dominated the pop charts; besides the successful singles and LP there were four-track EP collections of previously released songs, beginning with 'Twist And Shout', which made the top 5 of the charts (a previously unheard of achievement for an EP record), 'The Beatles Hits' and 'The Beatles (No. 1)'. In August a new single was issued by Parlophone entitled 'She Loves You', which entered the chart at number 2 the week after release, sold over a million copies in Britain alone and was the best-selling record of the year.

The British entertainment industry was centred on London and, not surprisingly, the Beatles and Brian Epstein soon moved there from Liverpool. The NEMS office was in Argyll Street in Central London; John and Cynthia moved into a flat in Kensington; George and Ringo shared a flat together in Mayfair, in the same block as Brian Epstein; and Paul McCartney lived in the house owned by the parents of his actress girl friend, Jane Asher.

In the autumn a new word, 'Beatlemania', was introduced into the English language by journalists to describe the fanatical enthusiasm of Beatle followers; behaviour which exceeded anything previously seen or heard in support of a British pop act. According to Brian Epstein, 'Ever since their beginning at the Cavern, I had known that the Beatles would become major stars, but no-one was prepared for the extraordinary events of late autumn 1963.'

During the year the Beatles made a number of appearances on British TV, most notably the Saturday teatime pop programme called 'Thank Your Lucky Stars', but on October 13th they made their debut on the most popular TV variety show of the time, 'Sunday Night At The London Palladium', attracting an audience of 15 million viewers. The front pages of the national newspapers next day carried stories of fans rioting outside the theatre from which the show had been televised live.

After a short tour of Sweden, the Beatles were back in London for an even more important televised concert. The Royal Variety Performance, held on November 4th, was attended by Queen Elizabeth the Queen Mother, Princess Margaret and Lord Snowdon, plus hundreds of rich and important dignitaries.

45

Police attempt to deal with teenage fans outside the London Palladium while the Beatles rehearse inside for a TV show. (Syndication International)

John Lennon introduced one song by asking, 'Would those in the cheap seats clap their hands, the rest of you can rattle your jewellery.'

Later, Lennon would recall, 'I was fantastically nervous, but I wanted to say something just to rebel a bit, and that was the best I could do.' It was perfect – a remark which typified both the Beatles' irreverent attitude and also the refreshing good humour that made them so popular.

The *Daily Mirror*'s one-word front page headline next day was a huge 'Beatlemania', above a story which began, 'You have to be a real sour square not to love the nutty, noisy, happy, handsome Beatles ... How refreshing to see these rumbustious young Beatles take a middle-aged Royal Variety Performance by the scruff of their necks and have them

Beatling like teenagers ... They're young, new. They're high spirited, cheerful. What a change from the self-pitying moaners, crooning their lovelorn tunes from the tortured shallows of lukewarm hearts.'

The newspapers began following the Beatles everywhere and soon discovered that John was married with a young son, a revelation which did not cause the group to lose any fans, though Cynthia continued to remain very much in the background. She saw John only infrequently, because his life as a Beatle had become a seven-days-a-week occupation.

The enormous amount of attention being focused on the Beatles by the press and fans put considerable pressure on the four young men, but they seemed to keep their sanity remarkably well, retained their freshness and originality, and continued to make good records, which kept improving all the time.

Two weeks after the Royal Variety Performance, 'With The Beatles', their second LP, was released. It topped the album charts the following week and even made the best-selling singles list, a somewhat bizarre and unorthodox feat.

The LP represented excellent value for money: fourteen new tracks that hadn't previously been available as singles. There were five more of the Beatles' favourite American songs, including 'Roll Over Beethoven' and 'Please Mr. Postman', infectious dance numbers which also served to draw the attention of British record buyers to the work of (then little known) American performers like Chuck Berry and The Miracles.

George Harrison made his debut as a writer, with 'Don't Bother Me', but the majority of the songs were from the pens of Lennon and McCartney and it was their material which won the highest praise from the music critics.

Perhaps the most surprising and unexpected critical acclaim came from *The Times*, whose classical music critic, William Mann, described the Beatles' songs in terms that they found almost impossible to understand. 'One gets the impression,' he wrote, 'that they think simultaneously of harmony and melody, so firmly are the major tonic sevenths and ninths built into their tunes, and the flat submediant key switches, so natural in the Aeolian cadence at the end of 'Not A Second Time' (the chord progression which ends Mahler's *Song Of The Earth*)'. Lennon and McCartney, he concluded, were 'the outstanding English composers of 1963'.

Despite the complexity that some saw in the Beatles' songwriting, 'With The Beatles' was in many ways a very simple work. It was recorded in one day and featured just George on lead guitar, John on rhythm, Paul on bass and Ringo on drums, plus George Martin playing keyboards on three tracks.

Martin took a vital role in the production of Beatle records, although he has always played down his contribution, creating the right kind of studio atmosphere and helping the four musicians to arrange their songs.

'My main role was picking out introductions,' George Martin said later, 'choosing a place for the solo, and its length and ending. I'd say "OK chaps, this is what we do for an opening, and this is where George does something on his guitar . . ." It was as simple as that, and that's how it worked out.'

George's 'simple' guidance was of considerable

importance to the success of the Beatles' records. Also important was the variety of their material, which was caused by their different tastes; Paul liked softer, more melodic songs, while George and John preferred heavier, more rocking music. 'The contrast in our tastes,' John said once, 'I am sure did more good than harm, musically speaking, and contributed to our success.'

The freshness and originality of the Lennon and McCartney songs was also a vital ingredient of their hit-making formula. Their complete lack of formal music training meant that they came up with ideas that music scholars would never have considered. As George Martin explained in his book, *All You Need Is Ears* – 'The ability to write good tunes comes when someone is not fettered by rules and regulations of harmony and counterpoint.'

Two weeks after the release of 'With The Beatles' came a brand new single, 'I Want To Hold Your Hand'. It was their fifth single, another number 1 and another million-seller. EMI were so confident that it would be a best-seller that they pressed 500,000 copies before the official release date. 'I Want To Hold Your Hand' eventually became the most successful song of all and Beatles authority Neville Stannard has estimated that the total world sales (in single, EP and LP form) are 21½ million copies.

Everything the Beatles touched seemed to turn to gold. Up-and-coming London band the Rolling Stones recorded John and Paul's 'I Wanna Be Your Man' and were rewarded with their first Top 20 hit; Liverpool group the Fourmost hit with 'I'm In Love', a Lennon and McCartney song that was never recorded by the Beatles; likewise 'Love Of The Loved', a Top 10 hit for

Cilla Black, and 'A World Without Love' by the duo Peter and Gordon (Peter was Peter Asher, brother of Paul's girl friend Jane).

Despite the successes, the Beatles were not earning an enormous amount of money in these early days, largely due to Brian's inexperience, because he charged too little for their services and was slow in renegotiating their EMI recording contract which only earned them a tiny fraction of the sale price.

But this same inexperience caused him to attempt and succeed at things more knowledgeable managers would never have tried, the Beatles' 'invasion' of America in February 1964, which was planned by Brian, being an excellent example. Up to this time few British pop acts had been successful in the US and most music industry people would have advised Brian to concentrate on the UK and Europe, but not to bother with the vast American market.

When George Martin had sent 'Please Please Me' to his opposite number at Capitol Records in Los Angeles, he'd been told, 'We don't think the Beatles will do anything in this market.' But Brian wasn't to be put off and flew to America where he found a concert promoter, Sid Bernstein, who was willing to take the financial risk of booking the Beatles into the famous New York concert hall, Carnegie Hall. Next Brian persuaded Ed Sullivan, the popular TV variety host who'd played a key role in launching Elvis Presley on to the unsuspecting American television audience in 1956, to book the Beatles. That booking was enough to convince Capitol that they should release some Beatle records and spend some money on publicising them.

'I Want To Hold Your Hand' was the record which

Above: *The Beatles step off their plane at London Airport after returning from their American tour. Behind them are Brian Epstein* (left) *and Derek Taylor* (right). (Syndication International)

Below: *The Beatles arriving in the American capital, Washington, by train.* (Syndication International)

'broke' the Beatles in America. Released by Capitol just before Christmas, it began picking up radio play in January and quickly became a popular favourite on several stations. The Beatles had spent Christmas and the New Year giving 'The Beatles Christmas Show' at a London theatre, visited France for some concerts, and then on February 7th flew to the United States. 'I Want To Hold Your Hand' was close to the top of the charts and the visit couldn't have been better timed.

New York teenagers were offered a free T-shirt if they went out to Kennedy Airport to meet the Beatles and over 3000 took up the offer, screaming hysterically when the group and their entourage arrived, thereby causing chaos and pandemonium and ensuring that this first visit to America got off to a wild and crazy start. The Beatles were instantly front-page news across the US.

Four air-conditioned Cadillacs took them to the smart Plaza Hotel in New York where the management were shocked and dismayed at the crowds they attracted, and offered to pay for them to stay anywhere else, but the group had moved in all their luggage and were unwilling to move.

There was a press conference when the Beatles gave few sensible answers, a complete reversal of the way popular entertainers normally behaved.

'What about the movement in Detroit to stamp out the Beatles?' asked one person.

'We have a campaign to stamp out Detroit,' came the reply.

'What do you think of Beethoven?'

'I love him,' said Ringo, 'especially his poems.'

The Beatles' appearance on the Ed Sullivan TV

show attracted an audience of 70 million, 60% of the potential viewing audience. According to Beatles' biographer Philip Norman, 'On that night, America's crime rate was lower than at any time during the previous half century. Police precinct houses throughout New York could testify to the sudden drop in juvenile offences.'

The Beatles' first American concert was at the Washington Coliseum. The British Ambassador, Sir David Ormsby Gore, held a reception for them at the British Embassy, which turned out to be the one unpleasant part of their visit – the upper-class British guests treated the Beatles like museum objects and when one woman went so far as to cut off some of Ringo's hair for a souvenir, the four musicians wisely left.

Back in New York they played two very successful concerts at Carnegie Hall, and could have filled the hall several times over, such was the demand for tickets. Then they flew to Florida for a couple of day's relaxation on a beach and another Ed Sullivan TV show, broadcast from a Miami hotel, where the technicians told reporters that the Beatles were the most cooperative and friendly performers they'd ever worked with.

The sales of Beatle records in America now went through the roof. All the early releases which Capitol had turned down were soon racing up the charts. By the end of March, the Beatles had all Top 5 singles, and seven more songs were also listed.

5

A Hard
Day's Night

The Beatles returned to England to begin work on their first full-length feature film, 'A Hard Day's Night', at Twickenham Studios in early March. They had managed to take a few days off in America, but seemed in no hurry for a longer break or holiday, preferring instead to get on with the job of being Beatles.

Their schedule for the rest of 1964 would be hard and punishing, but they seemed genuinely to enjoy working under pressure. The Beatles had four very different personalities but were good friends and worked well as a team, though this was as much due to their shared goals as anything else.

Each had to make concessions adapting to the wishes of the others for the sake of group unity, though John Lennon, always the rebel Beatle, would later recall arguments, particularly with Brian Epstein who insisted that they conform on several things, including the wearing of identical suits on stage.

'In the beginning it was a constant fight between Brian and Paul on one side and me and George on the other,' Lennon remembered. 'I didn't dig that and I used to try and get George to rebel with me, I'd say to him, "Look we don't need these suits, let's chuck them out of the windows." '

But he did conform most of the time, like the others, because they were all enjoying their success and wanted to be even more popular. Some years later John confided that their main ambition was to be bigger than Elvis Presley, who had been the undisputed 'King' of popular music since 1956.

'We reckoned we could make it because there were four of us,' said John. 'None of us would've made it alone, because Paul wasn't quite strong enough, I didn't have enough girl appeal, George was too quiet and Ringo was the drummer. But we thought that everyone would be able to dig at least one of us, and that's how it turned out.'

The pressures would mount as the originality of what they were doing faded, they became increasingly popular and then virtual prisoners of their own success, but in early 1964 being a Beatle was still fun for much of the time.

Even while filming 'A Hard Day's Night' they found time for other activities, including appearances on TV programmes like ITV's 'Ready Steady Go', and recording the soundtrack album that would be released with the movie. The songs had been written quickly and at odd moments – sometimes between shows, while travelling, even on the beach in Florida while sunbathing; but were still good.

'A Hard Day's Night', originally planned as 'Beatlemania' but re-titled after a catch phrase that Ringo was always using, was the perfect vehicle for expanding their popularity, by presenting their music and amusing personalities to the international audience.

The black and white film was a semi-documentary, directed by Dick Lester from a script by Liverpudlian Alun Owen, who actually invented some Beatle words, like 'grotty' (for grotesque) which passed into common usage after the film was shown. 'A Hard Day's Night' followed the Beatles for thirty-six hours, on a train journey from Liverpool to London and then preparing for a TV show. It was full of quirky camera angles and ingenious cinematic tricks that were perfectly suited to the offbeat humour of John, Paul, George and Ringo.

The Beatles were natural performers and whenever the rather thin plot sagged there was always another song. Premiered in London on July 6th, and the next month in the United States, 'A Hard Day's Night' was a great success with both critics and public.

It was also, significantly, much better than any of the films Elvis Presley was making in Hollywood. He was in a rut, making a series of very similar films in which he inevitably played a happy-go-lucky all-American boy, and, though doing good box-office business, was losing his fans and popularity in the pop world.

By 1964 the Beatles had already taken over from Elvis in many ways. They were selling more singles and LPs than anyone since Presley's arrival on the scene eight years before, and they were changing the face of popular music. Just as four-man pop groups with long hair had suddenly emerged in Britain during 1963, so the American scene was changing; some bands even taking English-style names to cash in on the Beatles' popularity.

Their American success was repeated in other countries around the world, including Australia, where there were six Beatle singles in the Top 10 in March 1964. A specially recorded German version of

'I Want To Hold Your Hand', 'Komm Gib Mir Deine Hand', went quickly to the top of the West German charts and stayed there for several weeks.

John Lennon, meanwhile, was satisfying an important need for a little individual recognition away from his fellow Beatles. In late March, his first book, *John Lennon – In His Own Write* was published by Jonathan Cape.

It was a collection of his eccentric writings, the kind of things he'd been doing since childhood, mostly silly stories with words changed for comic effect. *In His Own Write* included such gems as 'The Wrestling Dog', 'The Fingletoad Resort Of Teddiviscious', 'The Moldy Moldy Man' and 'No Flies On Frank'. They were illustrated with his own spidery drawings and, like his songs, had been written at odd moments between shows and recordings.

The critical acclaim for his nonsense writings was quite extraordinary. 'To tell you the truth,' John said later, 'they took my book more seriously than I did myself. It just began as a laugh for me.' By the year's end 300,000 copies had been sold and another book, *A Spaniard in the Works*, had been commissioned.

Lennon certainly deserved recognition for his comic gifts, but some of the praise and comparisons with great English writers like Lewis Carroll were excessive. He was an amusing writer, but had far greater talents in writing and performing songs.

The Beatles' hits kept coming; March saw the release of another new single, 'Can't Buy Me Love', which went into the British shops with a million sales already guaranteed from advance orders, while over two million copies had been reserved in the United States. The theme song from 'A Hard Day's Night', released in July, and 'I Feel Fine', which appeared in November, completed a trio of million-selling number 1s in 1964.

Two albums were recorded by the Beatles during the year; 'A Hard Day's Night', which was their first LP of original songs, went straight to the top of the best-sellers and stayed there for twenty-one weeks, finally being toppled by 'The Beatles for Sale', in December, which featured a collection of Lennon and McCartney originals plus more cover versions of their favourite American songs.

While his charges were filming and recording, Brian Epstein was trying to cope with demands for the Beatles to play in almost every country in the world outside the Eastern bloc. He was probably under far greater pressure than the individual musicians and at least once during the year considered takeover offers for his company and the group, but in the end stayed at the helm of NEMS.

He enjoyed many aspects of running such a successful company and was particularly pleased when the spotlight shone on him. He'd become something of a minor celebrity and was a recognisable face to a large proportion of British newspaper readers. He conducted some interviews for an American TV company, was profiled by the BBC for the prestigious 'Panorama' programme and wrote (with the help of publicist Derek Taylor) a book entitled *A Cellarful of Noise* all about himself and his acts, which was published in November.

Following the completion of filming in May, and before a strenuous tour of Europe, the Far East and America, the Beatles went abroad for a short holiday; Paul and Ringo to the Virgin Islands with their girl friends Jane Asher and Maureen Cox, while John and George went to Tahiti with Cynthia Lennon and Patti Boyd, the latter an actress George had fallen for during the shooting of 'A Hard Day's Night'.

The Beatle girl friends suffered harsh treatment whenever they had the misfortune to run up against jealous fans, and both Patti and Maureen had been shoved and kicked on separate occasions, but Cynthia, on her rare public appearances, was treated with respect, partly because she'd known John before he was famous and also because they were married.

The period from June to November was a blur for all the Beatles. They visited the far corners of the world but had little or no chance of sight-seeing, simply experiencing a mind-numbing succession of airport departure lounges, identical-looking hotel rooms, and the seedy back-stage areas of large stadiums and concert halls.

Concerts in Scandinavia, Holland, the Far East, Australia and New Zealand were followed by a month of concerts in the United States. They travelled across America in a private jet to vast concert arenas which were unsuitable for playing and listening, but ideal for satisfying the huge demand for tickets. The poor acoustics were actually irrelevant as the loud screaming made it very difficult for anyone to work out what was being played, unless you had an intimate knowledge of the records, could spot a familiar word or chorus, or recognised Paul's bass line.

It was an unfortunate phenomenon of the sixties that pop fans screamed hysterically throughout the performance of their favourite singer or group, though since the seventies even the most popular acts

59

have been allowed to perform their music in relative quiet. Nobody could derive much pleasure from listening to the music at Beatle concerts, which were more like celebration parties for the fans at being so close to their idols.

In the week of August 5th 1964, 'A Hard Day's Night' was number 1 on the singles and LP charts in both Britain and America, a very rare feat. Two weeks later they reached the Hollywood Bowl for one of the most famous concerts they ever gave, which was recorded and released as an LP record several years after they'd split up. Numerous VIPs, including the singers Frank Sinatra and Dean Martin, tried unsuccessfully to get tickets. The towels used by the Beatles after the show were cut into tiny pieces, stuck on certificates and sold as 'Beatle Souvenirs'.

It was just one of many clever marketing ideas which made a fortune for the makers, though the Beatles saw little of this money that was earned by using their name, due mainly to Brian Epstein's inexperience in the field – he'd given away the marketing rights for a very low percentage of the profits early in their career.

But the Beatles did now have plenty of spending money and used every opportunity to buy; dashing into shops to make purchases before they were spotted and mobbed by the fans. They loved buying clothes, trinkets, jewels and adult toys – like movie cameras.

John was the first Beatle to buy a house of his own. In July the Lennon family moved into a mock Tudor house in Kenwood, near Weybridge, Surrey, which was a very rich neighbourhood. They had a swimming pool and John quickly arranged for the installa-

The Beatles live on stage. Left to right: *George, Paul and John. Ringo is obscured from view.* (Syndication International)

tion of a small recording studio. Cynthia and Julian Lennon (now aged one) lived there all the time, but John was an irregular visitor, invariably away touring or at the EMI studio in London.

When he did come home he'd often stay up all night, writing and doodling, playing records by his favourite American singer, Bob Dylan (who was to

John with his first wife, Cynthia, and son, Julian. (From *The Beatles* by Hunter Davies)

become a very important influence on his writing), then sleep late into the day. Julian Lennon grew up hardly knowing what his famous father was really like.

Soon after the move Freddie Lennon, John's father, turned up like a bad penny working in the kitchen of an Esher hotel not far from Weybridge. He sold his life story to a weekly magazine and made a record, called 'That's My Life', which was considered by most people to be taking an unfair advantage of his son.

John and Freddie met and the meeting is not thought to have been very friendly, but John gave his father some money and later helped him to get a flat of his own. 'I didn't want to see him,' Lennon recalled later. 'I was too upset about what he'd done to me and my mother and that he turned up when I was rich and famous and not bothered turning up before.' Freddie continued to see his son from time to time, until his death in 1970.

John was very generous to his family and close friends. In 1965 he bought his Aunt Mimi a bungalow in Poole, Dorset, and also set up his boyhood friend, Peter Shotton, in business, paying £20,000 for a supermarket.

In October and November, the Beatles toured the British Isles, and didn't play to a single empty seat, the demand for tickets far exceeding the supply everywhere. In December they rehearsed for the second of the Beatles' Christmas shows in London, which ran into January.

December also saw the release of 'Another Beatles Christmas Record', a 7-inch flexidisc which was sent to all 65,000 members of the Beatles Fan Club. It was an annual tradition, begun in 1963 and continuing until 1969, for the group to make a short record of messages to their fans with snatches of singing; 'Jingle Bells,' 'Happy Christmas' and a piece of nonsense entitled 'Can You Wash Your Father's Shirts' were featured on this one. The members of this largest fan club in the world also received regular news of their idols in *The Beatles Monthly*, a glossy magazine.

The year 1965 opened with Brian Epstein and the Beatles planning their schedule for the whole year: a second feature film, again to be directed by Dick Lester; a tour of Europe and another visit to the US, including a show at the Shea Stadium in New York which would be the largest outdoor concert in history; and the recording of two more LPs and some singles.

Their new film, 'Help!', was considerably more time-consuming, ambitious and expensive than 'A Hard Day's Night'. It was shot in colour, featured actors who had made their names in fashionable TV satirical programmes and involved exotic locations like the Austrian Alps and the Bahamas.

The plot centred on the efforts of an oriental priest to obtain, by any means, a very precious and sacred ring, which had somehow found its way on to one of Ringo's fingers. One of the most amusing and memorable aspects of the film was the Beatles' living accommodation. Each was seen to enter adjoining and very ordinary-looking terrace houses, but once inside it was revealed to be a huge single apartment with a sunken bed, an organ that rose up from the floor, and a wall full of vending machines dispensing food and drink.

The film was made at the time the world's press was full of stories about 'Swinging London'; articles about the bright, young and famous people who were responsible for big changes in the worlds of music, fashion and the arts, and had come to prominence at the same time as the Beatles. Dick Lester's film, with flashy and bewildering photography, many strange camera angles and strip cartoon effects, fitted the times perfectly.

'Help!' was bright, colourful but also very superficial, just like all the 'Swinging London' stories. One effect was to make the film look old-fashioned and out-of-date within a few months, though it was very well received in the summer of 1965, did excellent business and provided the Beatles with another massive international hit – the single and LP of 'Help!'. But the euphoria surrounding the movie was to be short-lived and would put the Beatles off making films as a group for quite a while.

The British premiere of 'Help!' was attended by the Queen's sister, Princess Margaret, and her husband, Lord Snowdon, who made no secret of their enthusiasm for the Beatles. Another 'fan' was the new British Prime Minister, Labour leader Harold Wilson, who was another Liverpudlian. He was delighted to be associated with the Beatles, the working-class heroes who had risen to fame and fortune from his home town.

At Harold Wilson's instigation, the Beatles were awarded with the MBE (Member of the Order of the British Empire) in the Queen's Birthday Honours List in June 1965, in recognition of their achievements for Britain. The announcement caused a furore of protest and several MBE holders complained, some even sending their awards back to Buckingham Palace. The Beatles themselves were very surprised;

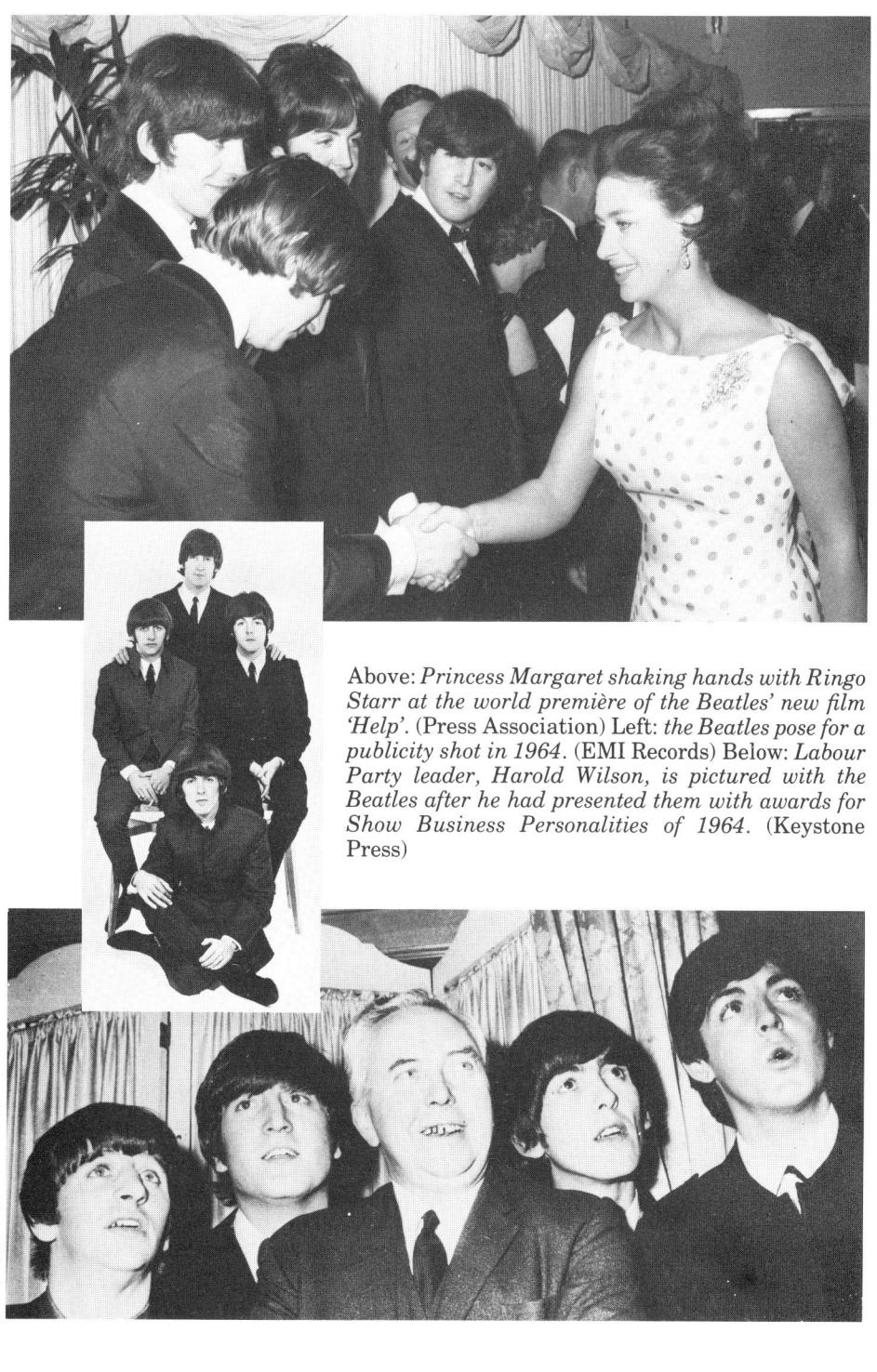

Above: *Princess Margaret shaking hands with Ringo Starr at the world première of the Beatles' new film 'Help'.* (Press Association) Left: *the Beatles pose for a publicity shot in 1964.* (EMI Records) Below: *Labour Party leader, Harold Wilson, is pictured with the Beatles after he had presented them with awards for Show Business Personalities of 1964.* (Keystone Press)

'I thought you had to drive tanks and win wars to get the MBE,' said John.

Their investiture with the MBE by the Queen at Buckingham Palace in October was one of the Beatle highspots of the year. Another was the historic concert at New York's Shea Stadium, before 56,000 screaming fans, and later a TV audience of many millions. The show grossed $300,000 and the Beatles had to be escorted from the stadium in an armoured Wells Fargo van, for their own safety.

In the autumn, the Beatles worked on their sixth British album, 'Rubber Soul', which featured some of their finest work. They'd become very skilled at the business of making records and now controlled everything, from the design of the album, the choice of title, the recording and all the material. 'We were getting better, technically and musically,' recalled John. 'In the early days we didn't even know how you got more bass.'

By now John and Paul were writing all their songs separately, only helping each other out with the odd word or phrase, but compositions were still jointly credited. 'Rubber Soul' contains four of John's best and most personal songs; 'Norwegian Wood (This Bird Has Flown)', a song about his affair with another woman, though disguised so that Cynthia wouldn't understand; 'Nowhere Man', which he had written sitting on the steps of his house at Kenwood after his mind had gone blank and he'd felt like a 'nowhere man sitting in his nowhere land'; 'Girl', which was about John's dream girl; and the nostalgic 'In My Life', a song that would take on a particular poignancy after Lennon's death.

6
Sgt. Pepper

At the start of 1966 the Beatles were top of the world; the most popular group in entertainment history, whose every record shot straight to number 1 wherever there were pop charts. They'd been awarded honours galore, even from the Queen of England, and everyone seemed to love them.

But for John, Paul, George and Ringo, life as Beatles was losing a lot of its early glamour. The novelty of fame and fortune had worn off and some aspects of their work, particularly the concerts and touring, had become very tedious and tiresome. Leading a normal life, doing things like shopping or walking in public parks, had become impossible because of the dangers of being mobbed by over-zealous fans.

The year was a turning point in many ways and each had periods when they wished they weren't Beatles and actively pursued independent projects away from the others. They also had to cope with a lot of criticism, including a particularly harsh and vicious campaign in America, and music writers who suggested that they might be losing their 'magic touch'.

John had many moments of uncertainty during the year; he'd later describe it as his 'what's it all about period', as he questioned his own ability to write and perform. He was eager to change but unsure where to turn and therefore grabbed any chance of temporary escape from the increasing pressures in his life. Drugs provided the quickest escape route and he took many LSD 'trips'.

LSD is an illegal hallucinatory 'mind-expanding' drug which can give the taker ecstatic highs or suicidal lows. It's regarded today as a generally unpleasant and dangerous drug, but in the mid-sixties it was very new and fashionable, and the dangers were less well known.

John's LSD experiences were often depressing, but he found they helped him to experiment with new sounds and songs and he spent many hours in studios playing with tape loops and distorting noise. The Beatles' 1966 album, 'Revolver', contains some of the early results of these experiments, including the song 'She Said, She Said', which recalled a frightening LSD trip with an American actor who kept repeating 'I know what it is to be dead', and 'Tomorrow Never Knows', the LP's puzzling final track which was supposed to sound as if it was 'coming from a hilltop in Tibet'.

The results were both fascinating and annoying for Beatle fans but proved to be particularly influential on other musicians, and in the following year there was an explosion of psychedelic rock from people trying to interpret their drug experiences through music. It was a particularly self-indulgent period of rock which produced several superstars of the future though relatively little music of lasting quality.

Where it had been John who provided the outstanding songs on 'Rubber Soul', it was Paul who wrote most of the highlights of 'Revolver', including

'Here, There And Everywhere', 'For No One' and the classic song about loneliness, 'Eleanor Rigby'. 'Revolver', which was released in August, featured cover art by the Beatles' German friend Klaus Voorman.

Germany was the first stop on what would be their final world tour, beginning in June. They played in Hamburg, where John told the support group, 'Don't try and listen to us, we're terrible these days', and took time out to visit some of their old haunts. Then they flew to the Philippines for concerts where they unintentionally snubbed the President by not turning up for a reception and were subsequently given a very unpleasant time by the authorities.

Their next foreign trip, to America, was far worse. They arrived to a raging controversy over remarks made by John Lennon in an interview with Maureen Cleave of the London *Evening Standard* some months before. During the interview John was talking frankly about religion, 'Christianity will go,' he'd said. 'It will vanish and shrink. I needn't argue about that. I'm right and I will be proved right. We're more popular than Jesus now. I don't know which will go first – rock 'n' roll or Christianity. Jesus was all right, but his disciples were thick and ordinary.'

The remarks caused little comment in England, but the US they were taken out of context by a magazine and it was reported that John had boasted 'We're bigger than Jesus now'. There was a savage wave of angry demonstrations, particularly among right-wing religious fanatics in the American south, including ritual burnings of Beatle records, photos and souvenirs.

John attempted to apologise, 'I'm sorry I opened my mouth,' he said at an American press conference. 'I'm not anti-God, anti-Christ or anti-religion.' But the controversy and threats continued throughout their American trip and extended overseas, including South Africa where the government banned the playing of Beatle records on the radio for five years.

They hated the last tour of America; the halls were vast and impersonal, and the screaming of the fans meant they couldn't hear what they were meant to be playing. 'There was no pleasure in playing any more,' John said later, 'not like in the old days.'

There was also the problem that wherever they went people wanted to meet them. The fans could usually be kept at bay, but it was difficult to say 'no' to requests from local dignitaries, or to handicapped people. 'On our last tour,' John told a journalist on his return to England, 'people kept bringing blind, crippled and deformed children into our dressing room. Mothers would say, "Go on, kiss him, maybe you'll bring back his sight." Now we're not cruel, we've seen enough tragedy in Merseyside, but when a mother shrieks, "Just touch him and maybe he'll walk again," we want to run, cry, empty our pockets. We're going to remain normal if it kills us.'

So the Beatles stopped touring, concentrating their musical energies exclusively on their recording activities, spending longer and longer in the studio. EMI were making a huge profit from international sales of Beatle records and allowed the group to use Studio 2 at Abbey Road whenever they wanted to.

The individual Beatles each devoted time to leisure pursuits and independent projects. Paul McCartney took time off to compose the music for a British film called 'The Family Way', George Harrison spent several weeks in India learning to play the sitar, an

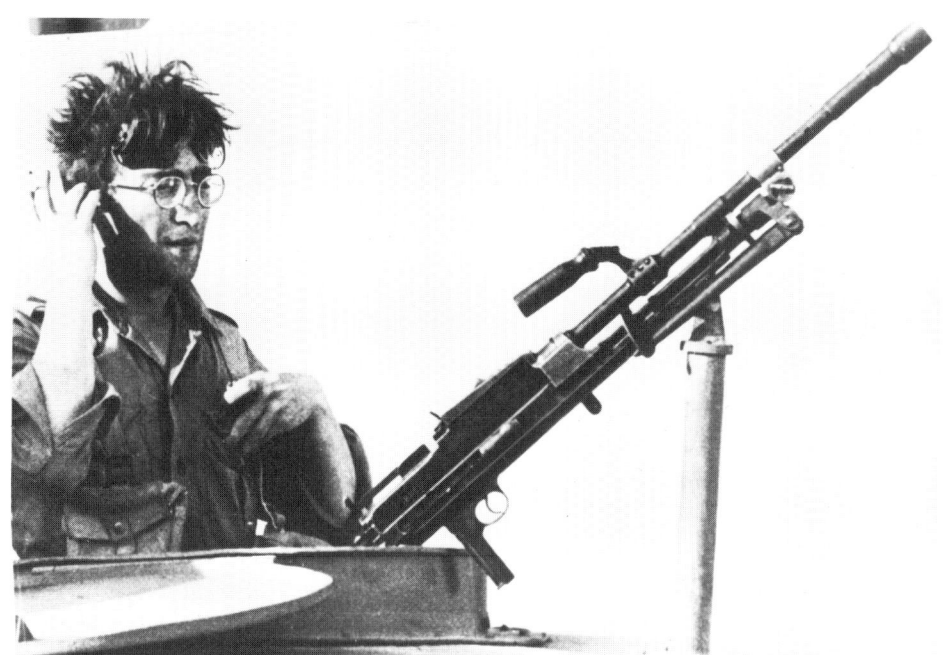

John Lennon as Private Gripweed, from the film 'How I Won The War'. (Daily Express)

Indian instrument which he'd first strummed during the filming of 'Help!'; and John made a film.

Despite his misgivings about 'Help!', Lennon chose to work again with Dick Lester, playing a serious, non-musical role as Private Gripweed in the anti-war film, 'How I Won The War'. The film received a poor critical reception when it was released in 1967; generally dismissed as misguided and ill-conceived, though Lennon received praise for his acting skills. John didn't particularly enjoy the making of the film, but it was further evidence of his willingness to try new activities.

This open-minded attitude caused John to accept an invitation to visit a new exhibition at the London avant-garde art gallery, Indica, in November. There he met Yoko Ono, a controversial Japanese artist whose work was on display.

Yoko, who was seven years older than John Lennon, was a gifted woman from a rich background – her father had been governor of a bank in Tokyo. She had moved to New York in her late teens and gradually built a reputation for her 'happenings', which many people found laughable and ridiculous, but which won praise from radical art critics.

At one of her New York exhibitions visitors were invited to set fire to blank canvases and 'watch the smoke'. John was quite entranced with Yoko and her exhibits, which at the Indica gallery included an ordinary apple on a podium and strange instructions at the top of a pair of step-ladders.

John and Yoko became good friends and over the next eighteen months they kept in touch, most often by letter, and Yoko delighted in sending him cryptic messages, like 'breathe' and 'keep laughing for a week'. 'Those letters kept coming and driving me

The Beatles – Ringo, John, Paul and George – in the costumes they wore for the 'Sgt. Pepper' album cover. (EMI Records)

mad,' John recalled later, 'but it was great too.' In 1968 their friendship would develop dramatically and they'd begin a creative and loving relationship which lasted as long as John's time in the Beatles, so the Indica Gallery meeting is now seen as important in his life as the Woolton Church fete where he first met Paul McCartney.

In 1967 the Beatles made the album for which they are still best remembered; the influential 'Sgt. Pepper's Lonely Hearts Club Band'. It was also the year in which they began a temporary infatuation with Eastern mysticism and their manager, Brian Epstein, died tragically.

The Beatles spent four months and some £25,000 making 'Sgt. Pepper', a far cry from the days of their early albums which were recorded and mixed within twenty-four hours and featured fairly simple songs and the basic instrumentation of guitars, bass, drums and occasional piano.

Producer George Martin was asked to come up with a mind-boggling assortment of instruments and special effects for the record, including a Victorian steam organ for 'Being For The Benefit Of Mr Kite', a harpsichord for 'Fixing A Hole', farmyard animals and a pack of foxhounds in full cry for 'Good Morning, Good Morning', and a large orchestra, in Paul's words 'freaking out', for 'A Day In The Life'.

The album was extravagantly packaged, unlike anything that had come before, though inevitably much copied since. There was a gatefold sleeve, a coloured inner bag holding the record, and a cardboard sheet of cut-out characters. The cover was a work of art; a montage of the Beatles, dressed as the imaginary Sgt. Pepper's bandsmen, surrounded by waxwork dummies (including their own likenesses from London's Madame Tussaud's) and photographs of many famous people.

The flamboyant nature of the album, the colourful design, the fairy-tale quality of the songs about bandsmen, circuses and the magical 'Lucy In The Sky With Diamonds', were all in keeping with the prevailing mood of young people in 1967.

It was the year of the hippie 'flower power' movement, based on the concepts of love and peace, which had begun in San Francisco and spread quickly across America and over the Atlantic to Europe. 'Sgt. Pepper' provided the theme music for the self-styled 'beautiful people' in their summer of love.

The music critics loved 'Sgt. Pepper' for the brilliant and varied song selection and the breathtaking sound effects. It sold like no other Beatle album before, topped the British charts for twenty-one weeks and was, until 1971, the best-selling LP of all time.

'Sgt. Pepper' can be said to have changed the course of rock music. Previously the seven-inch single had been the most important record of the music business, in terms of sales and prestige, but now groups and singers concentrated on making twelve-inch albums, following the Beatles' lead in crafting songs together around a common theme or subject. It also coincided with a major change in American radio as stations which played the Top 40 hits lost ground to those that featured hit album tracks.

In retrospect the LP seems uneven and not perhaps the Beatles' finest work, spoiled by weak tracks like George Harrison's self-indulgent 'Within You Without You', and since the late seventies critics have tended to choose either 'Revolver' or 'Rubber Soul' as the band's masterwork.

Nevertheless 'Sgt. Pepper' does contain some of their greatest material, notably songs written by John, including two which ran into trouble with radio stations because of supposed drug references; 'Lucy In The Sky With Diamonds', which was actually about a painting by Julian Lennon, though the initials (which spelt LSD) were asking for trouble, while 'A Day In The Life' ended with the words, 'I'd love to turn you on', which was a term used by drug takers.

The individual Beatles all admitted to drug use during interviews in 1967, notably LSD and marijuana, and all signed a petition for the legalisation of marijuana, but in late August they hit the headlines by becoming involved with the Eastern guru, Maharishi Mahesh Yogi and then announced at a press conference that they'd given up drugs.

Their involvement with the Maharishi, a hippie guru who questioned the values of Western society – the work ethic, competition and the importance of material possessions – came about through George's wife, Patti Harrison, who had joined the Spiritual Regeneration movement in February and then persuaded her husband and other Beatles to hear the group's leader speak in London in August.

They were very impressed by the Maharishi and his talk of achieving 'inner peace' through transcendental meditation, something they were all seeking as an escape from the pressures of fame, but which also tied in with the ideas of the hippie movement. They eagerly accepted his invitation to a five-day indoctrination session at a college in Wales.

The press followed and treated the whole affair as if

The Beatles and friends, including Rolling Stones singer Mick Jagger, with the Maharishi Mahesh Yogi in Bangor, Wales. Jagger is on the extreme right next to George Harrison. (Syndication International)

it was a huge joke, asking the Maharishi mocking questions, although the Beatles, dressed in kaftans and Eastern-orientated clothes, rushed to his defence and gave very serious answers – an interesting change from their original press conference style when the press asked sensible questions and they were flippant.

This extraordinary session was interrupted by the tragic news that Brian Epstein had been found dead in his London home. He had died of a drug overdose, possibly committing suicide, which he'd apparently tried twice before. Epstein, it was revealed, had become very depressed and dependent upon drink and drugs. While the Beatles merely toyed with illegal

76

stimulants, Brian had become hopelessly addicted to pep pills.

Brian had become very rich because of the Beatles – the *Financial Times* had estimated his wealth at about seven million pounds – yet he was ultimately unhappy. He led a bizarre lifestyle in his final years, sleeping by day and waking at night, frequently gambling, which he loved.

His moods of depression had much to do with the Beatles. Since they'd given up touring they hardly

Brian Epstein. (Syndication International)

needed his advice or organisation. There were many rumours before his death that the Beatles were considering dropping him.

Brian desperately wanted to get involved with the creative side of the business, and many thought that his secret ambition had always been to be one of the Beatles. Yet his attempts at record production failed and his lavish plans for venturing into London's theatre-land flopped badly. George Martin later recalled a recording session when Brian tried to tell John what to do during the recording of a Beatle song, but had been sharply put in his place with John's comment, 'You stick with the percentages, Brian, we'll look after the music.'

After Brian's death the Beatles entered a phase of confusion which led to bitterness, recrimination and the eventual dissolution of the band. It's unlikely that Brian could have held them together had he lived, but his death marked a turning point, after which things started to go wrong for the Beatles.

7
The
Apple Years

There were only a couple of months left to run on the Beatles' contract with NEMS Enterprises when Brian Epstein died, and when the renewal date came up the group decided to stick with the organisation they knew, which was now run by Brian's brother Clive, rather than go looking for a new manager, though it was made very clear that in the future the Beatles would play a far bigger role in their own management.

The Beatles' big summer hit of 1967 was the song 'All You Need Is Love', a genuine Lennon and McCartney collaboration which they had been asked to write and perform for an historic TV show – the first attempt at a worldwide satellite broadcast which involved countries in five separate continents and over 40 million viewers. Their simple and straightforward message to the world, 'All You Need Is Love', went out on June 25th, when they sang to a pre-recorded backing track and were assisted vocally by pop music friends including Mick Jagger and Keith Richards of the Rolling Stones and Keith Moon of the Who. The single version of the song went straight to number 1 in the British charts on the first week of release.

Their first hit single of the year had been a double A-side – Paul's 'Penny Lane' and John's 'Strawberry

Fields Forever'; which recalled places from their childhood in Liverpool. Though now regarded as one of their finest singles, it was significant as the first Beatle record to fail to reach number 1 since 'Please Please Me', stopping short at number 2. The last Beatle hit of 1967 was Paul's 'Hello Goodbye' which had been recorded whilst the group were making their very own film, 'The Magical Mystery Tour'.

This film was the first indication the public had of how chaotic things were to become for the Beatles without the guiding hand of Brian Epstein. They had resolved to make their own film as a result of their disappointment with 'Help!', after which one Beatle had told a reporter, 'We can make a better movie ourselves.' This turned out to be a somewhat ambitious statement because of their lack of experience.

The period from September to November was a particularly crazy one for the Beatles and their entourage. They set out each morning in a convoy of vehicles to film sequences of 'The Magical Mystery Tour' in the British countryside. Locations were rarely visited in advance and most of the shooting was improvised from a sketchy script.

Paul was the most enthusiastic about the film, though the others took turns at taking charge during the filming and editing stages which inevitably caused more chaos. The shambolic storyline revolved around a coach full of people on a 'Mystery Tour' which has been taken over by four magicians. When it was shown on BBC2 on Boxing Day it disappointed the fans and brought howls of derision from the critics, including a writer from the *Daily Express* who summed up the feelings of many when he described it as 'blatant rubbish'.

Visitors to Liverpool can still find the gate posts to the old Salvation Army Children's Home which inspired John's song 'Strawberry Fields Forever'. (Richard Wootton)

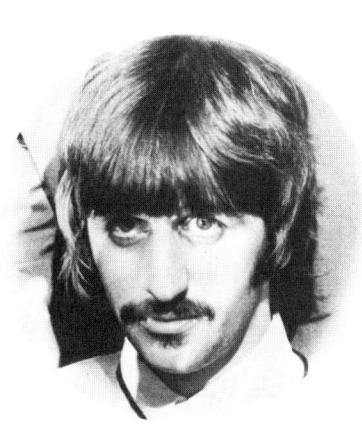

These photos were taken in 1967 for a BBC film, though John, Paul and Ringo are wearing the collarless jackets that were part of their image in the early days. (EMI Records)

The Beatles issued a double EP of the music from the film which, though it sold well enough, was also disappointing. There were only two songs of any lasting quality; Paul's 'Fool On The Hill' and another of John's quirky, experimental pieces, 'I Am The Walrus', which was full of amusing but nonsensical lines like 'Sitting on a cornflake, waiting for the man to come,' and some bizarre special effects which included part of a radio broadcast of Shakespeare's play *King Lear*.

At about the same time as the film making, the Beatles hit upon the idea of forming their own company, which became known as Apple. It began when John had a meeting with his old friend Peter Shotton and asked him to help run a clothes shop in London, because, 'We've got to spend two million pounds or the tax man will get it.' While Brian Epstein was

Crowds and police outside the Beatles' boutique on the day all the stock was given away.
(Popperfoto)

alive the Beatles made no attempt to avoid paying their huge tax bills, but they'd now been advised to be more organised with their very considerable wealth.

They hired some trendy fashion designers, who called themselves 'The Fool', and paid them £100,000 to design the Apple boutique at 94 Baker Street, in the heart of London, including the painting of a vast psychedelic mural of a Red Indian on the outside wall. Above the shop were the offices where several Apple companies were to be located – for films, electronics, publishing and the Apple record label which would be distributed by EMI and feature Beatle records and those of their 'discoveries'.

In the next few months a large amount of money was lost through these various enterprises, most of which were ill-conceived and staffed by people whose main concern was to line their own pockets. The shop was a total disaster which attracted many sightseers, several thieves but few genuine customers.

After months of watching their money and clothes vanish, the Beatles decided to close the Apple shop in July 1968. John announced that 'The Beatles are tired of being shopkeepers,' then gave away all the remaining stock to passers-by, which attracted large crowds and photographers from the world's press.

Many people thought that the Beatles had gone mad, because of their curious business activities and continuing enthusiasm for the Maharishi, who taught that material possessions were worthless and persuaded each Beatle to donate a quarter of his income to the Regeneration Movement.

In February 1968 they travelled to his Academy in Rishikesh in India for several weeks of religious studies and transcendental meditation. With them went several other pop personalities who'd been attracted by the little Eastern guru, including Mike Love of the American group the Beach Boys and the actress Mia Farrow.

The Beatles' interest and enthusiasm for the Maharishi collapsed while they were in India and they returned to London somewhat disillusioned, where Paul told reporters, 'We made a mistake, we thought there was more to him than there was.' When the puzzled Maharishi asked John Lennon why the Beatles were leaving the Movement, he replied, 'You're the cosmic one, you ought to know!'

Back in England, the Beatles threw themselves into their business activities, moving to bigger and better offices and employing a larger staff. A five-storey Georgian house at 3 Savile Row was the new Apple address and its features included a recording studio built in the basement by a self-styled electronics expert named 'Magic Alex', which never worked properly.

The Beatles set up the Apple Foundation for the Arts which dispensed grants to writers and artists, and they told an increasingly incredulous press that they wanted to use their wealth to help others. 'We want to see if we can get artistic freedom within a business structure,' said John. 'To see if we can create things and sell them without charging three times the cost.'

Only one of the Apple business ventures was ever successful; the record label. The first release was the Beatles' eighteenth British single, 'Hey Jude', which Paul had written about John's son Julian, and it topped the charts in late March, to be replaced by the second Apple release, 'Those Were The Days', by a

Welsh singer named Mary Hopkin, who'd been signed and produced by Paul.

The Beatles were under contract to make another feature film, but it was agreed that a full-length cartoon film would be accepted if they provided the music. The film, 'Yellow Submarine', featured the Beatles as cartoon characters defending the fictional Pepperland from music-haters like the Blue Meanies. The film had little to do with the real Beatles and actors were employed to provide the voices.

The soundtrack album, which wasn't released until early 1969, featured only a handful of Beatle songs, including three 'fillers' which had been written very quickly and at the last minute, plus some instrumental tracks by the George Martin Orchestra. This is one of the least successful records featuring Beatle music, not surprisingly considering the lack-lustre contents, but the film, which featured several Beatle classics from earlier LPs, was an artistic and box office success.

John's marriage to Cynthia collapsed in 1968 when his friendship with the Japanese artist, Yoko Ono, suddenly developed into a strong love affair and an intense creative partnership. Cynthia was saddened by the sudden end to their marriage, but was not unduly surprised and adopted a very philosophical attitude, as she explained in her autobiography, *A Twist of Lennon*, 'I don't blame John and Yoko. I understood their love. I knew I couldn't fight the unity of mind and body they had for each other. I had after all subconsciously prepared myself for what happened.' She filed for a divorce, which was granted in November.

John and Yoko's relationship became a big news story and they remained in the public eye for months because of a series of controversial happenings which they staged in support of a campaign for world peace.

One of their first public collaborations was the 'Acorn Event', when they planted two ordinary acorns at the National Sculpture Exhibition at Coventry Cathedral, below a silver plaque which read ' "John" by Yoko, "Yoko" by John. Sometime in May 1968'. It was, said John, 'a symbol of East and West coming together.'

Many people, including the other Beatles, were puzzled by John's infatuation with Yoko, and his new-found enthusiasm for avant-garde art. They could not understand what he saw in this small, unconventional-looking woman who was several years older than him. Many of the Beatles' fans were cruel to the new woman in John's life, calling her unpleasant names and writing threatening letters, and some sections of the press were savage in their criticism of her artistic work.

But the more criticism that came in, the closer the couple grew together. They had actually a great deal in common, shared a deep concern for world peace, were non-conformists and had vivid and original imaginations. They became inseparable, dressing alike and, soon, looking alike too.

Writer Bob Woffinden has accurately pointed out that Yoko took on several important roles in John's life. Lennon had experienced three very strong relationships – with Stu Sutcliffe, Cynthia and Paul McCartney, but Stu had died, he'd grown apart from Cynthia because of his life as a Beatle, and the relationship with Paul had dissolved as both had developed different musical styles and tastes. Now Yoko took on the different functions previously served by Cynthia (wife), Paul (creative collaborator) and Stu (the artistic adviser and influence).

In July, eight years after leaving Liverpool Art College under a cloud, John Lennon had his first art exhibition, at the Robert Fraser Gallery in London. It was greeted with universally harsh words from the press. The show included dozens of charity collecting boxes and a huge white canvas with the words 'you are here' at the centre. At the opening, 365 white, helium-filled balloons were released, bearing the message 'You are here – please write to John Lennon'. Replies flooded into the address on the label, and most were uncomplimentary.

John was surprised, but commented, 'The trouble, I suppose, is that I've spoiled my image. People want me to stay in their own bag. They want me to be lovable. But I was never that. Even at school I was just called "Lennon". Nobody ever thought of me as cuddly.'

Yoko went everywhere with John, so was present when the Beatles got together at the EMI studios in May to begin work on their new album. There was already a great deal of material available, as John, Paul and George were going through a very creative song-writing period, so it was decided to release a double album, which at this time was very unusual in pop music.

Between May and October, some thirty tracks were recorded, each taking an average of thirty hours to cut and mix. The results were very varied and revealed just how much John and Paul had grown apart musically. Paul was composing songs that were very strong on melody while John's contributions were increasingly radical and experimental.

There were a lot of arguments, which caused Ringo briefly to quit the group, particularly when John criticised Paul's 'childish' lyrics, on songs like 'Ob-la-di, Ob-la-da', and McCartney responded by attacking Lennon's more outrageous offerings, like 'Revolution 9', a jumble of sound effects and noises which remains the longest (8 minutes 15 seconds) and least played Beatle track of all time.

Yoko created a tension which made Paul, particularly, feel uncomfortable, as he explained later, 'It became very difficult for me to write with Yoko sitting there. If I had to think of a line I started getting very nervous. I might want to say something like "I love you, girl", but with Yoko watching I always felt I had to say something clever and avant-garde.'

John's most interesting contributions to the LP included 'Happiness Is A Warm Gun', which attacked American gun enthusiasts; 'Sexie Sadie', a thinly-veiled criticism of the Maharishi, which included the line, 'You made a fool of everyone'; and two very personal tracks which didn't involve the other Beatles in any way, 'I'm So Tired' and 'Julia', the latter about his mother, which he wrote with help from Yoko.

Producer George Martin was more worried about the proposed double album and tried hard to persuade the Beatles to drop the weaker tracks and issue a very strong single LP, but they wouldn't agree.

The album was released in November. The cover, which an artist had been paid a lot of money to design, was plain white, though each copy had a small serial number stamped in black at one corner, while inside there were four glossy colour photos of each Beatle, plus a lyric sheet with a photo-montage of the musicians with their wives and girl friends. It was called 'The Beatles', but quickly became known as 'The White Album'.

Advance orders in Britain alone were 300,000. Despite the criticism of John and Yoko, the group remained enormously popular. By the end of the year the combined world sales had topped four million, and it was the biggest selling double album for several years, until its figures were surpassed by the 'Saturday Night Fever' soundtrack LP in 1978.

Meanwhile, controversy continued to surround John and Yoko. On October 18th the flat they shared in central London was raided by police and both were arrested and charged with the possession of marijuana. Despite John's frequent claims to have taken illegal drugs, it was the first time the police had attempted to arrest him. A few weeks later he appeared in court, pleaded guilty, and was fined £150.

In December, John and Yoko released an album of their experiments with tape and sound in a cover which was immediately banned by many record shops, because it featured the pair standing naked. EMI refused to distribute it and none of the critics had a kind word to say about the disjointed sounds, bird calls and screaming which made up the record. Sales were very low compared to normal Beatle records and most went to people who thought the controversial sleeve might some day become a collector's item.

Around the same time work began on a project

which would eventually surface as the Beatles' third and final feature film, 'Let It Be', the documentary of the making of an album, but also a distressing portrait of a great band falling apart. The four musicians were seen at their best, recording classic songs like 'The Long And Winding Road' and 'Let It Be', and at their worst, arguing and quarrelling.

On January 30th 1969, the Beatles went on to the roof of the Apple building in Savile Row with amplifiers and instruments and played a short set of songs – which was filmed and included in 'Let It Be'; watched by a small audience of local office workers and some local policemen who had been called to investigate complaints of noise from neighbours. It was the last time the Beatles ever performed together.

The Beatles perform on the roof of their building in Savile Row. Ringo is on the left playing drums, a bearded Paul plays bass, John is in the centre and George, with moustache, is on the right. (Syndication International)

8
Plastic Ono Band

John and Yoko thrived on publicity, but when they decided to marry they went to considerable lengths to keep the ceremony a secret. On March 20th 1969 they flew from Paris, France to Gibraltar, the tiny British colony at the southern tip of Spain, where they were married at the British Consulate before only a handful of witnesses, including Beatle assistant Pete Brown. Just as Paul McCartney had done when he was married, some eight days previously to American photographer Linda Eastman, no other Beatles were invited.

From Gibraltar John and Yoko flew to Holland where they held a 'bed-in' at the Amsterdam Hilton and invited the world's press to talk to them. Dressed in white robes, they sat on a huge bed and explained that they were spending seven days and nights in bed in support of world peace and to protest against violence of all kinds.

They were mocked by most of the visiting journalists, who treated the whole affair as a joke, but the couple were undoubtedly sincere in their beliefs and John made the best of the situation by explaining, 'The least Yoko and I can do is hog the headlines and make people laugh. I'd sooner see our faces in the paper than yet another politician smiling at people and shaking hands.'

Right: *John Lennon and Yoko Ono board a plane after their marriage in Gibraltar.* (Daily Express)

Below: *John and Yoko holding a press conference from their hotel bed in Amsterdam.* (Keystone Press)

John was hurt by some of the press comments, particularly descriptions of his wife as 'ugly', but he was generally a much happier person than he'd been in the mid-sixties, when he was often depressed and wrote songs, like 'Nowhere Man', which reflected confusion and a feeling of futility. Yoko had helped him feel much more positive about himself and given him confidence.

Anthony Fawcett, an art critic who was employed by John and Yoko at the time, explained later, 'Yoko's most important influence on John was in showing him that he was an artist, in the all-encompassing sense of the word, and that as such he could broaden his horizons in unlimited directions.'

Their public campaigns for peace continued and in April they tried to enter the USA for another 'bed-in', but John's visa application was rejected because of his drug offence, so they went to Toronto in Canada and held a peace event there. While in the hotel bed, John came up with the idea of a song called 'Give Peace A Chance', which he wrote, and then recorded with friends who came to see him.

Earlier in the month, John had gone into the EMI London studio with just Paul to make a new Beatles' single, entitled 'The Ballad Of John And Yoko', which detailed the couple's well-publicised adventures in song and echoed the press reactions with lines like 'she's gone to his head'. Though many people feared that he was going mad, there was no doubting that John Lennon still had a sense of humour and didn't mind laughing at himself.

The song was released as a single in late May and followed the previous Beatle hit, 'Get Back', to number 1. John and Yoko issued another LP of homemade tapes in May, which again fell largely on deaf ears, but the Toronto-recorded single, 'Give Peace A Chance', which was released on Apple Records under the name of the Plastic Ono Band, fared much better, rising to number 2 in the charts by July. The song, with its very simple and direct message in the chorus line, became popular with peace groups and was still to be heard at public demonstrations against nuclear weapons over ten years later.

Besides the Lennons' peace activities, 1969 was dominated by legal squabbles over money. All four Beatles had now become very concerned about the way their money was being eaten up, particularly through the ill-fated Apple organisation.

'It's been pie in the sky from the start,' John told *Disc* magazine. 'If it carries on like this all of us will be broke in six months.' In February, Lennon hired a controversial American music business executive named Allen Klein (who also managed the Rolling Stones) to try and untangle their financial mess, and he immediately began cutting back on the Apple staff and expenses.

Paul McCartney was distrustful of Klein and called in his future father-in-law, Lee Eastman, to do his own investigations. The pair were soon involved in bitter exchanges and arguments as they sought to unravel different ends of the Beatles' affairs, now almost impossibly tangled within a variety of companies and confusing situations, and complicated by poor accounting at Apple.

Allen Klein had battles with Capitol Records in the USA, EMI in London, Dick James, who'd sold Northern Songs and John and Paul's compositions without telling either of them, and NEMS Enterprises, now

John Lennon and Yoko leave the Apple offices in April 1969 after a meeting of the Beatles' bankers. Allen Klein can be seen over John's shoulder. (Daily Express)

under the control of Clive Epstein. He had some success in making more money for the Beatles, and also himself – as manager he took a 20% cut of their income.

Somehow, while all the legal arguments were going on, the individual Beatles continued to write and record fine pop music. They spent much of the time between April and August at the EMI studio in North London, working on their twelfth British LP, which they named after the street outside the studio, 'Abbey Road'. They posed for the album cover photograph on the pedestrian crossing outside the building, thereby making the crossing and Abbey Road one of the best known pop landmarks in the world.

John and Paul had several half-finished songs which they brought to the sessions, but whereas on previous occasions they'd have helped each other out to complete them, now they were hardly talking, so they recorded them as they were and ran them together for a surprisingly effective medley.

The 'Abbey Road' album was released in September 1969 to worldwide acclaim and massive sales – up to ten million by the end of the seventies, making it one of the best-selling records of all time. The stand-out songs included John's 'Come Together', two by George, 'Something' and 'Here Comes The Sun', and Paul's 'You Never Give Me Your Money', which reflected on the financial problems they were all going through. There was also a curious track called 'Because', which was written and sung by John and featured Yoko playing some Beethoven chords backwards.

In September, John accepted an invitation to appear at a rock 'n' roll revival concert in Toronto, where he put together an impromptu version of the Plastic Ono Band, featuring Klaus Voorman on bass, English guitarist Eric Clapton on guitar, drummer Andy White plus Yoko. The concert was recorded and an album subsequently released, called 'The Plastic Ono Band – Live Peace In Toronto'. John enjoyed

One of the last group photographs of the Beatles, taken in 1969. (EMI Records)

playing before a live audience again and said, 'I don't care who I have to play with but I'm going back to playing rock on stage, I can't remember when I had such a good time.' This comment turned out to be wishful thinking because the concert was just one of a handful of live appearances he'd subsequently make.

In October, John and Yoko released 'The Wedding Album', an extraordinary sight and sound souvenir of the event they hadn't originally wanted anyone to know about. It was a box set containing two LP

97

records, photographs of the wedding, press clippings and a photo of a piece of wedding cake.

A month later John made one of the most controversial decisions of his life when he retrieved his MBE from above the TV set at his Aunt Mimi's house and returned it to the Queen, with a note explaining that he was protesting about Britain's involvement in the war in Nigeria, British support for the American war in Vietnam and because the second Plastic Ono Band single, 'Cold Turkey', was going down the charts.

It seemed to many people a rather pointless and foolish thing to have done, particularly by adding a comment about 'Cold Turkey' (a harrowing rock song about the pain of recovering from drug addiction), and his long-suffering Aunt Mimi was among the most upset, telling a reporter soon afterwards, 'I share John's views about Britain's involvement in the Nigerian war, but I cannot agree that this is the way to register a protest. If I'd known what he wanted to do with it, I would not have let him have his MBE. This is all very much out of character for John.'

Lennon was confusing a lot of his friends and British fans by his outbursts and changeable behaviour, but in the USA and Canada his statements, particularly about world peace, were taken much more seriously. At the time many young people were caught up in an emotional campaign against the Vietnam war, which had cost the lives of many American servicemen and thousands of Vietnamese.

In mid-December John and Yoko flew to Toronto again and held press conferences where their comments about peace were taken on face value and without the mocking of the British and European journalists. They announced ambitious plans for a huge Peace Festival (which never materialised), were featured on coast-to-coast TV shows and then had an audience with the Canadian Prime Minister, Pierre Trudeau. It was inconceivable that the British Prime Minister would have given John Lennon a meeting at the time because of the furore about returning his MBE, but Trudeau welcomed the chance of meeting the controversial Beatle.

The Lennons were back in England for the dawn of the new decade and John was soon hard at work on a new solo album with the famous American producer Phil Spector. It was becoming increasingly obvious that John had lost all his enthusiasm for the Beatles and that the end of the group was in sight. He'd told Allen Klein several times that he was leaving, but it was Paul McCartney who made the break-up of the Beatles official.

In April, Paul released his first solo LP 'McCartney' and said that he was leaving the group, 'because of personal, business and musical differences', though everyone, including Paul, knew that it was John who'd caused the split – 'John's in love with Yoko and he's no longer in love with us,' McCartney explained soon afterwards. 'He wanted a very intense relationship with her; at the same time, we'd always reserved that kind of intimacy for the group.'

The Beatles would never work together as a foursome again, but their records continued to be issued, beginning a month later with the release of the soundtrack LP for 'Let It Be', which had the largest advance order of any LP in American recording history – over three million copies. Sadly, it was one of their weakest efforts. In the *New Musical Express*, critic Alan Smith described 'Let It Be' as 'A cardboard tombstone, a sad and tatty end to a musical fusion which wiped clean and drew again the face of pop music.' Subsequent Beatle releases were compilations of previously-issued material, with the exception of their in-concert album, 'The Beatles Live At The Hollywood Bowl', which had been recorded in the mid-sixties but wasn't released until 1977.

The recorded output of the Beatles until 'Let It Be' had been remarkably consistent; a collection of some of the finest and most influential pop music ever recorded, but in the seventies each Beatle made his own records and though all had varying degrees of success, none was able to maintain the same consistently high quality of performance.

Paul McCartney had the greatest commercial success, writing and performing several million-selling albums and singles containing likeable but unadventurous pop songs, none of which quite matched his best work with the Beatles.

Both George Harrison and Ringo Starr had big hits in the years immediately following the break-up of the group, but by the mid-seventies they'd lost much of their support and releases became infrequent.

For music critics and serious rock fans it was John Lennon who produced the most arresting and interesting records of all the ex-Beatles, though the quality ranged from the truly awful to a handful of compositions which matched his finest work in the sixties.

John went through many phases and changes with Yoko in the seventies, and these inevitably affected his work. They began the decade with a deep involvement with the work of the American psychiatrist

Arthur Yanov, author of the book *The Primal Scream*. From April to August 1970, John and Yoko stayed at Yanov's house in Bel Air, Hollywood and underwent personal 'primal therapy' with him.

He believed that most people's problems could be traced to something that happened in their childhood, and his technique was to 'take people back' to relive some of their unsettling childhood experiences. With John this meant re-living the rejection he'd felt because of his father's absence and his mother's indifference. Previously he'd blocked his feelings about childhood out, but Yanov helped him change that.

'He showed me how to feel my own fear and pain,' John said later. 'Therefore I can handle it better than before . . . It doesn't just remain in me, it goes round and out. I can move a little easier.'

The Lennons returned to England in the summer and their new home, Tittenhurst Park in Ascot, a magnificent eighteenth-century Georgian manor they'd bought the previous year for £150,000. Here John had installed a private recording studio and he continued working on his first solo LP. He played all the guitar parts and some piano and was helped out by Ringo on drums, Klaus Voorman on bass and the American musician Billy Preston on keyboards.

He was determined to write and record songs that were clear expressions of how he felt about himself and the world, in contrast to his work with the Beatles which he now thought had been restricted: 'We were all so pressurised that there was hardly any chance of expressing ourselves, especially working at that rate, touring and always kept in a cocoon of myths and dreams.'

The finished record, 'John Lennon/Plastic Ono

Band', which was released in December, was very direct, personal, honest and frequently painful, notably on tracks like 'Mother' and 'My Mummy's Dead' which concentrated on his troubled childhood, and 'God', where he expressed his disbeliefs – 'I just believe in me, Yoko and me, That's reality'.

Many people found the record too honest and open and there was little radio play, which limited sales. The best track, 'Working Class Hero', was a very personal song about John's feelings about being a performer. 'When I wrote "Working Class Hero" I was thinking about all the pain and torture that you go through on stage to get love from the audience who really despise you – in a subtle way,' he explained. 'They demand something from you. You go up there like Aunt Sally and have things thrown at you. It's idiots like me who go up there to get tortured.'

The same month John's solo album was released, Paul McCartney began high court proceedings to end all aspects of the Beatles' partnership, and to control Allen Klein. A judge ruled that a receiver should be appointed to handle the Beatles' income and that Allen Klein should have no more to do with the group.

The year 1971 opened with a remarkable interview between John Lennon and American writer Jan Wenner, being published in the magazine *Rolling Stone*. John's determination to be honest and open now spilled over on to the printed page and he revealed a great deal about himself and the Beatles which the public had never heard, including the seamier, unattractive side of life 'on the road', which must have made his former colleagues squirm uncomfortably.

John and Yoko's Georgian mansion – Tittenhurst Park. (Daily Express)

Lennon had been very pleased with his solo album but disappointed at its lack of exposure, so for the next record, 'Imagine', which he made during the summer of 1971 at Tittenhurst, he sugared the pill, sweetening the musical side but retaining the strong personal songs and radical messages.

The title track, 'Imagine', illustrates this perfectly; it's anti-religion, anti-convention and against the capitalist system, yet it sounded pleasant to all ears and was successful, becoming, after his death, the most popular and best-loved John Lennon song of all. 'Now I understand what you have to do,' he said. 'Put your political message across with a little honey.'

'Imagine' was one of his finest works, including other great songs 'Jealous Guy' and 'Oh My Love', plus a very savage attack on Paul McCartney's songs, called 'How Do You Sleep'. The LP was produced by Phil Spector and featured Klaus Voorman once again, plus George Harrison on guitar and Nicky Hopkins, a noted session musician, on keyboards.

9

Some Time in New York City

The Lennons' home at Tittenhurst Park was large and beautiful, but though the couple had enough money to buy anything they wanted and employed a small army of builders who worked on numerous alterations and improvements to both the mansion and the grounds, John and Yoko's life there was frequently dull and lonely. They didn't encourage people to visit them, had long periods with little or nothing to do and often spent whole weekends in bed.

'At that time in their lives,' wrote biographer Ray Connolly, 'they seemed almost like a middle-aged or elderly couple who were convalescing after an illness.' Their isolation led to depression and their relationship suffered, as Anthony Fawcett, one of the few friends who made regular visits, recalled later, 'When they were depressed, both John and Yoko would overreact to any little problem. Often I found myself in the middle of a heated emotional outburst which left me sad and disorientated.'

A change was needed and it came in the summer of 1971, when they moved to New York City, though the move was not a conscious decision at the time they left England. Yoko was trying to seek custody of her daughter, Kyoko, the child of her previous marriage to a man named Tony Cox. Her ex-husband had an annoying habit of disappearing with his daughter and, in August, John and Yoko pursued him to the Virgin Islands, and then on to New York. There was to be a protracted legal battle in the American courts and Yoko eventually won custody of Kyoko in March 1973, but Cox disappeared again and Yoko eventually left things as they were when it became obvious that the child wanted to live with her father.

On their arrival in New York, the Lennons stayed at the St Regis Hotel and soon realised that the city was the place where they wanted to live. They would never return to Tittenhurst Park, where they'd left workmen installing an artificial lake, and eventually the property was sold to Ringo Starr.

John loved the energy and activity in New York, which reminded him of his exciting early years with the Beatles in Liverpool and Hamburg. In London he was unable to lead a normal life because of the problems of being mobbed by fans – hence his retreat into the countryside and life as an eccentric recluse; but he found he could walk the streets of Greenwich Village in New York with little or no interference.

'America is where it's at,' he told Jan Wenner of *Rolling Stone*, 'I should have been born in New York.' John and Yoko moved into a two-room loft apartment in Greenwich Village and rented a studio in nearby SoHo, where they worked on various avant-garde art projects. In October, Yoko had an exhibition, entitled 'This Is Not Here', at a gallery in Syracuse, New York, to which John contributed as 'guest artist'.

The change, from the peace and quiet of his English mansion to the frenzied pace of New York City, was dramatic and, for a while, John was much happier. 'This city has become the centre of the artistic world,' Lennon told a British newspaper reporter. 'It's really great to live here with all these talented people. New York is at my speed. It's a twenty-four-hour-a-day city, it's going on around you all the time, so much so that you almost stop noticing it. I like to finish work in the studio at 4 am and go out and find it's all still throbbing.'

John had recorded songs and made public statements about social injustice and the need for world peace, but in New York he became actively involved with political protests. Several of America's best-known left-wing radicals, including Jerry Rubin and Abbie Hoffman, were soon in touch with him, welcoming the support and publicity that his name brought to any cause. John and Yoko supported a protest for American Indian rights at Syracuse, gave

John and Yoko in revolutionary-style clothing. (Apple Records)

a concert for the relatives of victims of a controversial riot at Attica prison, and played a benefit for jailed-activist John Sinclair.

In his enthusiasm to help people, John plunged into situations often without sufficient thought or understanding of the causes, some of which were considerably less worthy than others. Several people took advantage of him because they realised newspapers always took notice of the things John Lennon said. These highly-publicised activities in radical politics brought him to the attention of the US Government and led to innumerable problems with the granting of an extension to his Visitor's Visa to the USA.

It was 1972, the year of the American Presidential elections and Richard Nixon, the focus of most left-wing protests, was seeking re-election. Nixon's supporters feared that Lennon could seriously damage his chances of returning to office, so they sought to have the singer removed from the country.

The immigration authorities refused to extend his visa, explaining that it was due to John's drug record in England. But Lennon had money to hire powerful lawyers to argue his case and soon discovered the extent of the campaign to remove him from the USA.

John appeared on the Dick Cavett TV talk show on April 29th 1972 and astonished viewers by proclaiming that government agents were following him around and that his telephone was being tapped. Many people thought he was imagining things, but later it was proved to be true.

In 1974, a leading American newspaper columnist, Jack Anderson, discovered that Richard Nixon himself believed rumours that Lennon was involved in a campaign to stop him being re-elected, and that the British drug conviction was just an excuse being used to stop John saying anything in public. US Government papers released in 1983 revealed even more: FBI agents had followed Lennon in the months prior to the election in the hope of arresting him on a new drugs charge or otherwise 'neutralising' him so that he could be deported.

Lennon did not lead the public campaign that had been imagined by Nixon's men, nor was he deported, but the activities of the Government caused him considerable distress, expensive lawyers' fees and wasted time. He was ordered to leave America on several occasions, but each time lodged appeals.

John and Yoko teamed up with an American rock band called Elephant's Memory to record some protest songs for the album, 'Some Time in New York City', which also featured a bonus LP of live recordings made in England by the Plastic Ono Band in 1969. It was an unsuccessful record, both commercially and critically, and marks the low point of Lennon's post-Beatle recording career.

The songs, some solo efforts written by John or Yoko, others collaborations, were aggressive and simplistic and focused on several radical issues of the day, including women's liberation, the war in Northern Ireland between the IRA and the British army, and the imprisonment of left-wing activists, and they illustrated rather acutely Lennon's naivety and lack of understanding about many of the issues involved.

The press were harsh in their comments when the LP was released in mid-1972, including *Rolling Stone* which described the work as, 'Disastrous . . .

the politics are witless and the live jams mindless.'
John seemed to have forgotten his wise words of the
previous year about sweetening the message 'with a
little honey', and would later agree that the songs
weren't good – 'It became journalism and not poetry,
and I basically feel that I'm a poet.'

Despite the very cool response to the record, John
was still popular and a charity event at New York's
huge Madison Square Garden, featuring John, Yoko
and Elephant's Memory, was a great success, earning
a five-minute standing ovation for a concert which
included strong and impressive performances of the
songs, 'Give Peace A Chance', 'Cold Turkey', and
'Instant Karma', and raised a lot of money for handicapped children. It was one of several fund-raising
events involving the Lennons in the summer of 1972
which raised an estimated £700,000.

In December, John and Yoko had a seasonal hit
record in the UK with the beautiful 'Happy Xmas
(War Is Over)', which they'd cut soon after setting up
home in New York, with the Harlem Community
Choir. It was a very persuasive plea for peace and
remains one of the all-time great Christmas pop
songs.

In 1973, as his struggles with the immigration
authorities continued, John worked on a new LP,
'Mind Games', in which he attempted to return to the
more melodic and personal style of the 'Imagine'
album. The results, apart from the moderately successful title track, were not very impressive, but
made for easier listening than 'Some Time in New
York City' and, as he himself said later, 'It was like
an interim record between being a political lunatic
and back to being a musician again.'

109

The problems with obtaining his US visa and new legal wranglings over the Beatles' financial affairs – Allen Klein was now suing John, who in turn was suing Allen with Paul and George – made him depressed and contributed to his split from Yoko in October, after a relationship in which they had been almost inseparable, twenty-four hours a day, since 1968.

Stories about the break-up vary; at the time there were reports that one day John said he was going out to buy a newspaper and didn't come back, but Yoko was the dominant member of the partnership and it now seems that she wanted John out of her life, at least temporarily. In 1980, during a candid interview with *Newsweek* magazine, John explained, 'I was being an animal, and not considerate, and she rightly thought, "If that's the way you want to be, then not here with me." '

John flew to Los Angeles where he spent most of his time getting drunk with a group of musician friends, frequently making newspaper headlines after being ejected from clubs or involved in brawls. He later described the nine months on America's West Coast as 'one big hangover . . . it was hell.'

He had no desire to write new songs but went into a recording studio with Phil Spector, who'd been involved as co-producer on several of his solo projects, including 'Imagine' and 'Some Time in New York City'. John allowed Phil to take complete control of producing a rock 'n' roll album, featuring many of the fifties songs that he'd first performed at the Cavern Club with the Beatles. A host of name musicians were involved in the sessions which continued until there was a legal complication about the ownership of

John Lennon's former colleagues photographed during the seventies. Top: *Paul McCart-ney with his group, Wings, which included his wife Linda* (centre) *and Denny Laine* (left). Below left: *Ringo Starr.* Below right: *George Harrison.* (Photos EMI Records, RCA Records, WEA Records)

the tapes and Phil Spector disappeared, taking the recordings with him.

Confused and dazed, Lennon continued to hang around Los Angeles and was regularly drunk. He tried producing an LP with one of his drinking friends, the talented singer-writer Harry Nilsson, with help from Keith Moon, the notorious hard-drinking drummer from the Who. Lennon found the sessions a nightmare to control, but somehow an album, 'Pussy Cats', was completed and released.

John returned to New York in the summer. He cut down on his drinking, made preparations for court appearances in connection with his immigration case, and began work on a new solo album, 'Walls and Bridges', at the Record Plant studio in New York with musician friends, Klaus Voorman on bass, Jim Keltner on drums, Jim Ed Davis on guitar and Nicky Hopkins on piano.

The LP included some very personal material, including 'Nobody Loves You (When You're Down And Out)', which reminded listeners of his nine months of drunkenness; 'Scared', in which he worried about the advance of old age; 'Steel And Glass', a veiled attack on Allen Klein; and 'Whatever Gets You Thru The Night', on which he was joined on vocals by one of the most successful British singers of the seventies, Elton John. The same month he helped Elton to record a single version of the Lennon and McCartney song, 'Lucy In The Sky With Diamonds', which was released in November and became a very big hit.

Just before he started work on 'Walls And Bridges', John received the tapes from the rock 'n' roll sessions from Phil Spector. Listening to them in a sober state he found much of the material was poor and that many of the musicians were playing out of tune. He returned to the Record Plant studios in October with the same musicians from the 'Walls And Bridges' sessions, and re-cut some of the songs. The resulting LP, simply called 'Rock 'n' Roll', and featuring a cover shot of John from the Hamburg days, subsequently appeared in March 1975.

Elton John had made Lennon promise that if 'Whatever Gets You Thru The Night' became a number 1 single, he'd appear with him at a concert at Madison Square Gardens. John had never had a chart-topping hit as a solo artist in America and was very surprised when the record made it to number 1, but kept his promise and when Elton appeared at the New York concert hall on November 28th, Lennon joined him for 'Whatever Gets You Thru The Night', 'Lucy In The Sky With Diamonds', and then 'I Saw Her Standing There', which brought a wild reaction from the capacity crowd. It was John Lennon's last public performance.

Backstage, John met up with Yoko again. He had telephoned her frequently during their separation but they'd rarely met face to face. The meeting was the beginning of a reconciliation and in January 1975 they were living together in the Dakota building apartment which they'd bought shortly before the split. They would remain together, almost inseparable, until Lennon's tragic death in 1980.

10
Starting Over

After a year that had involved some of the most depressing and degrading moments of John Lennon's life, 1975 was a time of transition, when he overcame several problems, stopped making records and dropped out of public life.

On January 9th, the legal partnership of the Beatles, which had proved impossible to break up until their complicated financial affairs were sorted out, was finally dissolved. The years of arguments, angry words and bitter recriminations were over, and John was once more on speaking terms with his old friend and partner, Paul McCartney, though the pair met up with each other only occasionally.

John and Yoko were seen in public together again for the first time in March, when John was guest presenter at the Grammy Awards ceremony, and were photographed back-stage with stars David Bowie (one of the most successful British singers of the seventies and with whom John had worked on the 'Young Americans' LP in January), Simon and Garfunkel and Aretha Franklin.

Soon afterwards came news that Yoko was pregnant, which made John happy but also very concerned, because three times before Yoko had been pregnant and on each occasion suffered a miscarriage. John was determined that his wife should

John and Yoko in November 1980. (Geffen Records)

be as comfortable as possible and free of any worries, so they moved temporarily into the countryside.

John spent most of his time caring for Yoko, but was also continuing with his struggle to stay in America. In June he took action against the former Attorney General, John Mitchell, arguing that the deportation actions against him had been unjust, and in September was rewarded with temporary non-priority status because of Yoko's pregnancy. It was a sign that he was winning his fight.

Victory came on October 7th 1975, when the US Court of Appeals ruled that the British law under which John had been convicted of drug possession was 'unjust by US standards', overturned the order that John should be deported and then, astonishingly, praised the singer by announcing, 'Lennon's four year battle to remain in our country is a testimony to his faith in the American dream.' It would be another nine months before John was finally given the official status of a permanent resident, but his long struggle was over.

Two days later, on John's 35th birthday, Yoko gave birth to a son, Sean Ono Lennon, at the New York Hospital. It was a difficult birth, Yoko was then forty-two years old, but Sean, who weighed 8lb 6oz, was a very healthy baby. 'I feel as high as the Empire State Building,' John said afterward

For the next five years, John's family became all-important to him. Remembering how he'd been deserted in his own childhood, and feeling guilty about neglecting his first-born son, Julian, he spent an enormous amount of time with Sean. When he gave his first interview in 1980, to *Newsweek* magazine, he explained, 'I hadn't seen my first son, Julian, grow up, and now there's a seventeen-year-old man on the phone talking about motorcycles. I was not there for his childhood at all, I was on tour.'

John became a house-husband and Yoko looked after the business affairs, organising John's money with brilliance and making their Lenono company very successful with shrewd investment in property, land and dairy cattle. At one point in the late seventies, the Lennons owned a house in Florida, another in Long Island and five dairy farms, as well as several apartments in the Dakota building.

'I had the baby, but I'm not a good mother at bringing up children,' said Yoko, 'John loved to be with Sean all the time, so I got on with the business side of things and John ran the house.'

The arrangement worked well. 'I'm more capable of making bread and looking after Sean,' John said later, 'and she's more capable of taking care of bankers and lawyers and deals.'

John stopped making records, though at the end of 1975 organised the release of a compilation album of some of his hits and 'near misses', entitled 'Shaved Fish (Collectable Lennon)', which contained singles, like 'Give Peace A Chance', which hadn't previously appeared in LP form.

He was then without a recording contract, a situation which he relished because 'I'd been under contract since the age of twenty-two and I was always "supposed to", supposed to write one hundred songs by Friday, supposed to have a single out by Saturday.'

There was another lawsuit involving John in 1976, over the disputed ownership of the 'Rock 'n' Roll' LP and he chose to fight the case, eventually winning in March with $45,000 awarded to him by the judge for damages to his reputation.

On July 26th, John was finally given his Green Card, which allowed permanent residence in the USA, after a hearing when several notable Americans, including author Norman Mailer and film actress Gloria Swanson, gave testimony in his support. A lawyer from the Immigration Services said that the US Government no longer objected to his presence in America. 'It's great to be legal again,' John said afterwards.

It was his last public statement for over four years and he was rarely seen, choosing to spend most of his time at home, often in his small white bedroom in the Dakota building, a room where everything, from the walls to the furnishings, was white. He played endlessly with Sean, took hundreds of Polaroid photographs, watched TV, read and listened to tapes. He

117

almost never answered the phone but made occasional calls out. He became very health-conscious, adopted a macrobiotic diet and lost a lot of weight.

John and Yoko had no close friends, but several advisers. One, Eliott Mintz, would later explain, 'Neither of them had any friends because there was enough going on between them and they didn't need to see other people.'

Yoko placed great importance on seeking the advice of astrologists, numerologists and 'direction people', and would rarely make a business decision without checking that the signs were right.

Sean knew little about his father's life as a musician until one day he saw part of a Beatles' film on television at a neighbours apartment and came running into John, saying 'Daddy, you were singing! Were you a Beatle?'

The trio made occasional expensive trips around the world, frequently booking a block of first class seats so that they wouldn't be bothered by the public, who, if they ever got close to John, inevitably asked for an autograph and the same question – 'When are the Beatles going to get back together again?' – which was a topic of popular discussion but something John knew would never happen. 'It's like asking, "When are you going back to school?" ' he would say.

John and Yoko broke their long silence in May 1979 when they took out full-page advertisements in several major newspapers around the world, headlined 'A love letter from John and Yoko to people who ask us what, when and why.' It was a bizarre and puzzling document which talked about 'the Spring Cleaning of our minds' and ended with the statement, 'three angels were looking over our shoulders when we wrote this.' Many of John's fans now believed the rumours that Lennon had lost all his enthusiasm for making music and had dropped out of public life for good. But a comeback was just a year away.

In the summer of 1980, Sean was coming up to his fifth birthday and the start of school, and John knew that he'd have more time on his hands for his own interests. The inspiration to make a new record came when John and Sean were on holiday together in Bermuda, and Yoko was looking after business in New York.

John was at a disco when, as he later told *Rolling Stone* magazine, 'I suddenly heard "Rock Lobster" by the B52s (a talented new wave group from Georgia) for the first time . . . It sounded just like Yoko's music, so I said to myself, "It's time to get out the old axe and wake the wife up!" '

In the next three weeks, in a burst of creative energy, John and Yoko wrote about twenty-five songs, then went into the Record Plant studio in New York with producer Jack Douglas, who later explained, 'We recorded the material one for one. One of John's songs followed by one of Yoko's. We cut twenty-two tunes in all. John came loaded with energy. Yoko wasn't sure how her stuff was coming out at first, and then, the second week, when we got to her better material, she started to really groove and became confident about the direction of the recording.'

An LP was released, called 'Double Fantasy' and credited jointly to John and Yoko, on the new Geffen Records, following negotiations between Yoko and the label boss, David Geffen. The front

119

cover featured a close-up photograph of John and Yoko kissing, the back a picture of the pair standing impassively on the pavement outside their New York home.

John's contributions (like Yoko, he wrote and sang seven tracks) were the songs of a happy man – of love for his wife, 'Dear Yoko' and 'Woman'; love for Sean, 'Beautiful Boy (Darling Boy)'; daydreaming, 'Watching The Wheels'; and his return to making music with Yoko, '(Just Like) Starting Over'. They were warm-hearted songs but received a cool response from the critics, who missed the snarling anger and

This photograph, from the back cover of 'Double Fantasy', was taken very near the spot where John was shot, outside the Dakota building in New York City. (Geffen Records)

off-beat humour of the old John Lennon. But Yoko's contributions won the best reception she'd ever had – they were her most commercial recordings to date, and her avant-garde style, which had been ahead of the time in the early seventies, was now similar to a lot of the popular new wave music.

Lennon's cheerful new outlook on life took some getting used to, particularly as his lyrics went against the grain of most hit songs of 1980 and it was only later, after his death when they took on a special poignancy, that critics realised John's material on 'Double Fantasy' was among the best he'd made since the 'Imagine' LP.

The record was released in November, just after John's fortieth birthday, and he gave a series of in-depth interviews in which he talked enthusiastically about his enjoyment of family life, his pleasure in returning to music making, and his future plans with Yoko and Sean. He seemed as happy and contented as he'd ever been, but then came tragedy: on December 8th 1980, he was murdered outside his home.

His killer was a twenty-five-year-old American from Hawaii named Mark David Chapman, who had come to New York a few days previously. Chapman was a sad individual who had twice, reportedly, tried to commit suicide. He'd hero-worshipped John Lennon since childhood and had become totally obsessed by him; having married a Japanese/American woman because she reminded him of Yoko, and on quitting his job in Honolulu, had signed out with the name 'John Lennon'.

Chapman was outside the Dakota building at 5 pm on Monday December 8th, clutching a copy of 'Double

Crowds gather outside the Dakota apartment block within minutes of the tragic shooting.
(Syndication International)

Fantasy' and, when John and Yoko left the building to go for a recording session, he asked for an autograph, which John duly gave on the LP jacket.

Just under six hours later, at 10.50 pm, the Lennons returned from the Record Plant where they'd completed work on Yoko's recording of the song, 'Walking On Thin Ice'. Chapman was waiting for them. He came up behind John, shouted 'Mr Lennon!', took up a combat stance and fired all the bullets from a Charter Arms .38 calibre handgun.

John staggered into the Dakota building saying, 'I'm shot,' followed by a distraught Yoko, who called for help. Two police vehicles were on the spot in minutes and one rushed John to hospital, but it was too late, he'd been terribly wounded and had died in the back of the car. Chapman made no attempt to escape and was arrested standing on the pavement, beside the gun he'd dropped after the shooting, reading a copy of the novel *Catcher In The Rye*.

There were numerous theories as to why Chapman, a man who loved Lennon and his music, should have shot him dead. The most popular is that Chapman's obsession had become so overwhelming that he fantasised he was John Lennon, then wishing to destroy his fantasy self he found the only solution was to kill the real John Lennon. Chapman was judged to be insane and committed to an institution, for at least twenty years.

It was incredibly sad and ironic that John Lennon, who had done so much to promote the cause of peace, should be killed in such a stupid and violent way. His death shocked and grieved millions of people around the world. He had been a very important and influential figure, particularly to the teenagers of the sixties, most of whom, like Lennon, were now married with children. No-one had been mourned by so many people since the assassination of the American President, John F. Kennedy, in 1963.

Thousands of New Yorkers began a vigil outside the Dakota building, at West 72nd Street and Central Park West, bringing flowers, candles and pictures of Lennon. Radio stations around the world played his best known songs, notably 'Imagine', the Beatles' 'In My Life' and 'Give Peace A Chance', which were particularly appropriate. Even DDR-1, the radio station in East Berlin which hardly ever plays Western music, aired a lengthy John Lennon tribute with Beatle records.

Not surprisingly, the album 'Double Fantasy' and

123

the single '(Just Like) Starting Over', sold fast in shops and were soon at the top of the charts in several countries. In Britain, John's records would outsell everyone else's for over a month.

Ringo Starr rushed to New York to comfort Yoko, and so did John's eldest son, Julian. Many celebrities sent messages of sympathy. For the major rock names it was a time of sadness, also of fear that the shooting might provoke a spate of copycat killings. Fortunately this did not happen, but security was increased and several performers went into hiding temporarily.

At least two Americans committed suicide in reaction to John's death and Yoko issued a statement saying, 'I'm really so concerned. This is not the end of an era. "Starting Over" still goes. The eighties are still going to be a beautiful time. It's hard, I wish I could tell you how hard it is. I've told Sean and he's crying. I'm afraid he'll be crying more. But when something like this happens, each one of us must go on.'

Many people paid tribute to John Lennon, including Paul McCartney, who was quoted as saying, 'John was a great man who'll be remembered for his unique contributions to art, music and world peace.'

Entertainer Frank Sinatra said, 'It was a staggering moment when I heard the news, Lennon was a most talented man and above all, a gentle soul.' Bruce Springsteen, one of the major American stars of the seventies, was among those who went on stage on Tuesday December 9th and commented about the tragedy, saying 'It's a hard night to come out and play when so much has been lost. The first song I ever learned was a record called "Twist And Shout" and if

Carrying on . . . Yoko Ono and Sean Lennon at London Airport in November 1983. It was Sean's first visit to his father's home country. (Syndication International)

it wasn't for John Lennon, we'd be in a different place tonight.'

The editorial in *The Times* of London observed that John Lennon and his fellow Beatles, 'were not the first working-class youths with provincial accents to make an impact on British life, but their example enabled millions more to crack the barriers between the classes . . . Their example was the most influential.'

John's body was cremated on December 10th, without ceremony, but an international silent vigil was held, for ten minutes on Sunday December 14th, at the suggestion of Yoko. 'John loved and prayed for the human race,' she said, 'Please pray the same for him. Please remember that he had deep faith and concern for life and though he has now joined the greater force, he is still with us.' 100,000 people turned up in New York's Central Park for the tribute

125

at 2 pm. Similar vigils were maintained around the world, including one in his home town of Liverpool.

Yoko, the victim of so much hatred and anger in the early seventies, now received an enormous amount of support and encouragement, including over two hundred thousand personal messages. She bore the tragic loss of her husband, friend and collaborator with remarkable strength, courage and dignity.

In one of the few interviews that she gave in the days immediately following the murder, Yoko told Robert Hilburn of the *Los Angeles Times*, 'People say there's something wrong with New York, but John loved New York. He'd be the first to say it wasn't New York's fault. There can be one crank anywhere.' Then she explained that she and John had hoped to live until they were in their eighties, 'We even drew up little lists of all the things we could do for all those years. Then, it was all over . . . But that doesn't mean the message should be over. The music will live on.'

Index